WILDER
JOURNEYS

WATKINS
Sharing Wisdom
Since 1893

Edited by Laurie King & Miriam Lancewood

WILDER JOURNEYS

True Stories of
Nature, Adventure
& Connection

This edition published in the UK and USA 2023 by
Watkins, an imprint of Watkins Media Limited
Unit 11, Shepperton House
89-93 Shepperton Road
London
N1 3DF
enquiries@watkinspublishing.com

1 3 5 7 9 10 8 6 4 2

Head of Design: Karen Smith
Typeset by Glen Wilkins
Illustrations: Giles Herman @gilesillustration

Printed and bound in the United Kingdom by TJ Books

A CIP record for this book is available from the British Library

ISBN: 978-1-78678-742-2 (Hardback)
ISBN: 978-1-78678-763-7 (eBook)

www.watkinspublishing.com

CONTENTS

FOREWORD

For more than twenty years I've led teams into the wilderness and have witnessed first-hand the transformational effects of these adventures in nature. I've seen it change people of all ages and backgrounds: turning the timid into the confident, the addicted into the recovering and the lost into the intentionally wandering. Curious to understand what I was observing, I've spent a decade researching the psychology of why these wild journeys are so impactful on our wellbeing. The evidence is compelling; challenges in nature can help us heal, grow, build resilience, improve confidence, strengthen relationships, experience joy and find meaning.

However, if we are to act on this knowledge, we need inspiration too, and this is where this wonderful book comes in. The authors immerse themselves in wild journeys both overseas and close to home, and share their adventures with passion and honesty. Stories filled with the magical enchantment many of us can only find when in the wilderness, of feeling alive, connected and at peace. They discover healing and meaning and show us that no matter how insignificant we might have felt, we can all make a difference. These pages have also made me more deeply appreciate the moment when my own understanding of my place in the world changed.

I was 19 years old and travelling alone through Africa. I'd made it in an open boat along Lake Tanganyika to Gombe National Park where I spent time with a wild troupe of chimpanzees. At first, I had been careful to keep my gaze low so as not to threaten them but eventually I glanced up to make eye contact with a juvenile female. We both stopped and shared the moment, and I was overcome by a feeling of kinship. I found this surprising at the time, even though I knew that we shared more than 95 per cent of the same DNA, that we were cousins. Similarly, I couldn't explain how I experienced a feeling of coming home; on that day their forest had become mine too, not with a sense of ownership but more of a shared responsibility to it and to each other. As a teenager I knew something significant had happened, but I couldn't put it into perspective at the time. I just knew I had been nurtured by the experience but also that I needed to protect my cousins and our forest.

In reading this book I've recognized the significance of my own early experience in the revelations of others who have taken wild journeys, such as Hamza Yassin's and Celia Bull's animal kin and Rupert Marques's and Miriam Lancewood's deep feelings of belonging in the wilderness. It is inspiring and strengthening to read these moments of shared realization. We are awakened, transformed and connected in a way that is not possible without immersion in the great outdoors. In the wild we learn to take responsibility for ourselves but also for our environment, and this empowers us to protect what we care for. Our wellbeing and the health of our surroundings are inexorably connected. Indeed, as Gregory P Smith explains (see pages 115–27), his wild journey revealed a gentler way to live in the modern world, one that does not cause destruction to others or the ecosystem while at the same time leading him to a much richer existence personally.

However, humans have become an urban species and we are now more disconnected than ever from nature. We are destroying what we love – our bodies, minds and environment –

faster than ever before. It appears we live in a time when there is general dissatisfaction with the way things are and, worse, a sense of powerlessness to change it. But there is another way.

The authors are sharing their gifts of discovery. Revelations that allow us to put our own experiences into perspective. Wisdom that gives us inspiration for a better life and hope for a healed world. Just as our indigenous ancestors did, they are living adventurously in nature and sharing their knowledge.

Take their lead, go on a wild journey and find your lessons for an enriched life. If enough people were to read this book and follow its example, we would see more joy, more responsibility for ourselves and our planet, and, eventually, positive change in the world.

Belinda Kirk
Author of *Adventure Revolution: The life-changing power of choosing challenge*
Founder of Adventure Mind

INTRODUCTION

LAURIE KING AND
MIRIAM LANCEWOOD

We are both from an intellectual culture that treats "nature" as somewhat separate from the human world – kept at arm's length. The word "Anthropocene", so often used, refers to a culture and society that put humans at the centre, and gives a false impression that we are more powerful and less dependent on other beings than we actually are. This stems back a long way, to a time where ideas of culture and nature were separated in philosophy and religion. The very first written reference to this separation was *The Epic of Gilgamesh* in 2700 BC. Gilgamesh, originally from shamanic nomadic origin, built the first-ever city, called Uruk. After he built the walls, he suddenly felt separated from nature and realized his own mortality. He saw he could not endure the way nature does – for the forest represented an eternal rhythm. Without a direct relationship to nature, the people felt lonely and isolated, and any achievement felt rather irrelevant in the face of death. Rather than seeking a new relationship, Gilgamesh, like countless people after him, began to seek revenge on nature by destroying it.

This book is a collection of incredible stories of transformation and creativity from those who have been driven by their dissatisfaction with their culture or lifestyle. Many of them have been on extreme journeys, pushing themselves to their limits, to connect with the essence of their animal being. They followed their eco-anxiety, trauma or sense of calling into the wilderness. Others have changed their lives to align with their values, advocating a more ecological approach to life, or helping others to improve their wellbeing through outdoor practices. They are just ordinary people, with extraordinary stories of connection, healing and oneness.

The idea for this book came to Laurie after she met Roz Savage (page 104) and Ffyona Campbell (page 87). She was impressed and inspired by Roz's courage in rowing across three oceans solo, and Ffyona's commitment to walking the world for 11 years, beginning when she was 16 years old. Roz's prerogative was to raise awareness about the damage we are causing to the biosphere, and Ffyona was driven by her search for the truth. Laurie could see in the eyes of these women that they knew something she didn't, deep in their bones, and they seemed to have a relationship with the natural world that was beyond what she could imagine. Laurie was desperate to hear what these experiences had taught them and to share some of their wisdom with the world. So, she and Miriam came together and decided to compile a volume of incredible true stories about people's wild adventures and nature connection journeys.

In all of the unique and unusual experiences narrated in this volume, there are some common threads. In each story the will of a human being is met by the challenging forces of the elements and the rawness of existence. We see the humility that grows from the awareness of the fragility and tininess of human beings, as well as our reliance on non-human beings for our survival. For example, Sophie Sung-Bin Hilaire (page 28) explores vulnerability, danger and death amid the forces of Everest's climate. Roz Savage (page 104) experiences her smallness underneath the gigantic sky one night during her Pacific Ocean crossing in her tiny rowing boat.

We also see how relationships with the more-than-human world can heal old wounds. For example, Gregory P Smith (page

114) has an epiphany in the forest, which helps him resolve patterns of addiction and self-abuse. The forest, in effect, acts as his healing centre, both challenging him and holding him. Karen Darke (page 178) feels the relaxing and healing of a shoulder injury as she slowly rolls over the mountains of Chile, far away from the competitive environment she was used to as a Paralympic athlete. Jennifer Joosten-Brisk (page 130) takes refuge in an Italian mountain village to heal from trauma. Denise Rowe (page 168) and Celia Bull (page 194) also demonstrate the healing power of witnessing non-human beings.

Some of the authors have learned important lessons from people whose culture does not separate humans from other beings, who understand the importance of listening and have a deep reverence for the land in which they live. For example, Angela Maxwell (page 76) speaks of her interaction with bushman B, who helped her as she walked through the Australian outback. Traditionally many indigenous cultures do not separate humans and nature. In Ecuador, mountains and rivers have legal rights – legislation that was developed in keeping with the indigenous worldview of animism and mutual respect for all beings. Similarly, people relying on the land for subsistence and livelihoods would understand inherently the interconnectedness of all beings.

Many cultures have been destroyed by the same mechanisms that are reducing biodiversity. Many nomadic peoples have been resettled in unsuitable housing and separated from their ancestral lands, the places with which they have such connection and that hold such significance for their wisdom cultures. It's this very theme that Rupert Marques (page 148) follows, as he sees first-hand how the resettlement of the Batonga people separated them from aspects of their culture tied up in their relationships to land and place.

It seems, when we are very close to a non-human being, it is possible to see ourselves reflected back as we are all, in essence, made of the same stuff. The ecosystem is a mirror for us, and the very fact that we are damaging the environment shows that we are damaging ourselves. Hamza Yassin (page 88) sees himself in the white-tailed eagle chick that he spends eight weeks filming. Karl Bushby (page 46) becomes a caiman as he floats, camouflaged, down a river in the Colombian Amazon. Miriam Lancewood (page 12) sharpens her hunting instincts as she begins to rely on feeding herself in the wilds of New Zealand. We, as humans, are so similar to other beings – we all come from the same root. Yet many of us are so far removed from our animal instincts in our daily lives. The authors show that our primal instincts are always there but just need to be reawakened.

Probably the most important lesson from this volume is that the answer to feeling more connected to nature is very simple. Just like in a romantic relationship or friendship, the more quality time you spend together, the more you know each other and the more connected you feel. Our relationship with non-humans is just the same. The more we spend time immersed in the elements, away from our computer screens and central heating, the more we will realize we are connected already. There's not much more to it. The more time we spend getting to know other beings and the more we listen to them, the more we will be able to act in ways that are beneficial for all of us.

––––––––––

The authors in this volume are all wildly inspiring. They began their journeys from a place in which they felt there was more to life. Many were dissatisfied with their current lifestyle, situation or culture – and sought to change that. They are all stories of transformation. Yet transformation cannot happen without some adversity and, indeed, many of them show us how these raw and adventurous challenges have changed their lives.

We acknowledge that not everyone will want to challenge themselves in such extreme ways as in this book. Some of the authors would not recommend it, having been driven to those lengths by trauma or shame. We also realize that, for some, access to wild places and the equipment needed for survival there is easier than for others. Yet David Malana (page 64) shows us that outdoor adventures should be for everyone, regardless of colour, while Karen Darke (page 178) proves that physical disabilities don't always have to be a barrier. We hope that more organizations such as David Malana's Color the Water will emerge to make outdoor activities and adventure more accessible for everyone. For example, The Visionaries is an organization based in the UK that works with young people from inner cities in wilderness settings. We have listed projects and organizations at the end of the book for your interest (pages 209–10).

Overall, we hope that these stories will inspire you to delve into a deeper feeling of connectedness with the natural world and your own animal instincts, to go on your own journeys of (re)connection. We hope you might find ways to transform your own eco-anxieties, cultural frustrations and emotional difficulties. You may feel the pull to the wild, too, to form a relationship with non-human beings – whether that be the ocean, the wind, a mammal or a bird – and witness the inherent power and strength of this living planet. You may feel called to take people with you, to help others to access the healing capacities of encounters with non-human beings and elements.

It seems that going outside the comfort zone of the Anthropocene is something important – and perhaps it could also help us all to change the way we do things – as many of us will have to shake up our comfortable lives for the benefit of everyone.

As you will see, these quite intense true stories have been interlaced with poetry and wise words from professional and amateur poets, environmentalists and nature connection guides, for those who like metaphor and short interludes to break up the drama. For example, Selina Tusitala Marsh, a former poet laureate from New Zealand, has gifted us with a poem about her connection to the ocean, 'Sea Chants'. Lemn Sissay, the official poet of the 2012 London Olympics and chancellor of the

University of Manchester, speaks of his yearning for connection to the land in 'Gold from the Stone'. We also have book excerpts from eco-psychologists and philosophers Bill Plotkin and David Abram, to inspire connection to your wild, animal soul.

There are so many ways to express connectedness with the more-than-human world, and we encourage you to go and do something, or be somewhere, to help you experience deeper connection – and we also invite you to use your creativity to express what you learned there. The experience could be beautiful, it could be harsh, but it will always teach you something.

MOSI'S MOTHERS
ZENA EDWARDS

"The psychotic drowns in the same waters in which the mystic swims with delight."
— Joseph Campbell.

Deidra shows up frustrated, with wine
dry roasted peanuts and a playlist of tunes
on her phone we don't listen to …
she wants to talk, to curse a burning planet
for stealing her adopted daughter.

"Mosi keeps paraphrasing some Rousseau quote about insanity."

"Being sane in a deranged world is insanity itself."

"Yes. That one."

Her cheeks concave deeply as she sucks the third Marlboro
down to the stub.

"She says this gluing crystals to her hair clips.
Says Amethyst amplifies the electromagnetic pulses
of Mother Earth's messages."

Deidra rolls her eyes.

"I mean, what makes her so special?"

Moh has a thick afro, her skin is dark, her forehead proud
her Kenyan heritage strong
long slender arms tattooed with the words *"Keep The Mother Close."*
and *"Rebel With A Healing Heart"*.

Moh is seventeen loves to garden, eat strawberries and basil leaves
plucked with fresh fingers she has grown
with her soft smiling Grandfather, watching his blue veins
under translucent skin throwing slugs over the allotment fence.

"Both she and Dad are annoying Earth babies."

Deidra curses the urge to connect to nature
that skipped a generation
an attentive Mosi, since the age of three meant, for him,
someone was listening.

"Lockdown was awful," says Deidra

9 to 5 denied, disorientated, she quips
"9 to wine o'clock", squeezed through a tight laugh.

Deidra buckled under the weight of the lengthening silences
between herself and the mother-lost child, she picked out
for her big brave eyes
from a small rural village, east of Mancha in Kenya
to save her from drought and the devastation of deforesting.

"How do I get her back? She hates me."

"She does not hate you."

I am Deidra's only black friend
she confided in me the rescue mission
of a climate refugee child
I do not ask the details.

Moh called me when she passed her driving test
"First time, Auntie!"
She drove 4 friends to Glastonbury to place their bodies
along the ley-lines and chant for Hecate, Persephone and Ceres
to speak to her Kenyan Ancestors on her behalf
to call in the Earth Gods to meet the diggers with wrath
and melt the dams desiccating local crops
till land is dust.

Moh tells me, more so now than ever
she vows to learn her roots
plant trees in her Motherland
of the money she has saved for a flight
after lockdown 2 ...

Deidra sups from a moment's silence

I gaze into the cloying claret
tannin coats my tongue
with the bitter wisdom of seeds, skin and stem.

Today, do I say, a saviour is only as powerful
as the will of the supplicant?
knowing Moh is molten lava, calmly insistent
her passions burning through Deidra's coddling
which prefers first world simplicity
over the full truth about speeding climate shifts
halved by madmen – deadlocks in parliament
are a licence to keep hitting the snooze button.

              "You know she sprayed her hair green and purple?!"

Moh tagged me into that instagram post
April 22, Earth Day,
her mohican afro, tall and glittering, eco-disco
small white teeth proud of the green fairy wings
she'd made from young bamboo canes
and tie-dyed net stockings
a peace sign thrust to the front of the photo
"The Fae world is real! #connected."

Co-conspirator, I doubled tap to "like"
to love this whistle blower
of institutionalized baby boomer chaos
who unfurls, a firefly,
from the smouldering soil of its seasoning ashes
at the pace of forests rewilding.

Mosi's Mothers © Zena Edwards, 2023

Zena is a writer, poet, mentor and radical educator of Caribbean heritage.

She is founder and director of Verse in Dialog – an arts and engagement CIC that champions arts that serve climate and environmental justice, equity and decolonization, personal sovereignty and collective wellbeing.

Miriam is the author of international bestseller *Woman in the Wilderness* (2017) and *Wild at Heart* (2020). She met Peter Raine in India and together they travelled for years through Southeast Asia and Papua New Guinea, eventually arriving at Peter's home country, New Zealand. In 2010 they decided to live in the wilderness of the South Island. They moved around like nomads, slept in a tent, cooked on a fire and Miriam learned to hunt. Initially they had planned just four seasons, but it became seven years.

This piece is a memoir from the first year in the wilderness.

ONE DAY IN A WILDERNESS LIFE

MIRIAM LANCEWOOD

It was dark when I heard the first sound. I listened to a lone bellbird, who slowly wakened the world. Gradually the others began to join in, and there was a beautiful morning chorus. There was no wind and the forest was still, as if everything took a moment to listen.

When the music ebbed away, the first light emerged through the trees.

I silently zipped open the tent, for Peter was still sleeping. Taking my clothes, I quietly crawled out. My bare feet touched the mossy forest floor. I dressed while looking out at the sky.

Finally, I thought. It promised to be a sunny day after three days of rain. A little breeze had blown up. It brought fresh, clean air and there was no smell of moisture in the wind.

In the half dark I found my belt and bow. I tied my hunting belt with my knife around my waist, picked up my bow and quiver, and began to walk toward the top of the valley.

I found my way up through the forest. There were big old trees, covered in moss. Flowers and mushrooms. Little creeks and streams everywhere. The sun was now rising over the mountain tops, and everything was warming up. I walked past fallen logs that seemed to be smoking – the damp was spiralling upward to the sky. I smelled the tree ferns and their old fronds and tried to detect a scent of wild animals.

Where would goats go, I wondered? Surely not in the thick bushes I found myself in? Every sensible animal would go to the river to move freely over the big round rocks in the riverbed. I climbed down a steep bank covered in ferns and young trees, holding my bow in one hand while the other shielded my face from all the sweeping branches.

When I came to the valley floor I quickly moved into the shade, for I knew everything is more visible in the sunshine. The white rocks had been washed clean by thousands of years of pure water. My eyes fell on a shiny green stone. I picked it up and marvelled at the patterns inside. Nature creates the most perfect pieces of art, I thought. I wanted to take it home but instead I placed the green stone onto a big boulder. I had learned never to accumulate anything apart from bare necessities – because we had to carry everything we owned.

I followed the river upstream and only stopped when I saw a big patch of snowberries. I put my bow on the ground, kneeled, and ate as many berries as I could stomach.

Where are the goats? I thought, when I had finished my breakfast and set off again, following the edge of the forest. Stop thinking too much, I told myself, for animals can hear your thoughts. Let everything and everybody forget I am here.

Then I realized nobody in the world knew where I was, or was even aware of which part of the country we were in. We had no phone, no beacon, no machine of any kind, not even a clock. Nothing monitored in which valley we were. If we had died, nobody would have had any idea where to look for our bodies. This thought didn't make me afraid; rather I felt more alert, for I could not afford an accident.

I climbed up a big branch of an old tree so that the animals could not smell my scent. The wind would keep my whereabouts secret. I was in a huge river valley with forest on every side. Some tree ferns were growing in the lower valley, but it was mostly beech trees at this higher elevation.

From my viewpoint in the tree, I could look into the distance. The river was meandering down the mountain. Right below me was a smooth rock face, and a bit further on was a logjam with a little pool. Behind the dam were big round boulders, fallen from the mountain tops.

Snowberries for breakfast had filled my stomach, but after some hours roaming I felt hungry again. Food was on my mind all the time. What part of the animal shall I eat first? I imagined how happy Peter would be if I came back with a goat. We had not eaten meat for a week, and the wild animals were our staple food. If I failed, we would have to eat again the food supplies we had brought with us: rice and beans, and flour to make bread.

Since we had first set off into the wild – a year ago – I had mostly failed as a hunter. Consequently we had eaten beans every day. Peter did his best to make varied meals by adding many herbs and spices, but it was not easy to eat the same thing so often. Those first months I had tramped around for countless hours without seeing any animals. On the rare occasion that I did see some in the distance, they had smelled me and disappeared without trace.

I had come back, sometimes almost in tears – for not seeing any sign, or for shooting and missing, or for shooting and wounding, or for losing expensive arrows. I sat around the fire, silent and empty-handed. The predecessor of success is always failure, I learned.

Instead of hunting, in that first winter I had tried my best at setting traps for opossums. These were small marsupials – a nocturnal animal introduced from Australia. Without natural predators, this species had quickly become a so-called pest. Most people regarded them as rats, without knowing that opossums are very nutritious and tasty, too.

During the past year in the wilderness, I had learned to wait. And today this skill was used again. I sat very quietly in my old tree. The one who wins in the wilderness is the one with patience, I knew. The ability to wait is the ability to hunt.

The sun shining through the branches made beautiful moving patterns on the ground. A little breeze over the water turned the leaves ever so slightly. The leaves went from green to yellow and many colours in between, and all around me the scene was like a big moving kaleidoscope.

Maybe there are no wild animals here. Maybe I should have gone up that other side creek, I thought. Maybe I made the wrong choice. Maybe they had smelled me already. Doubt was overshadowing my mind.

I waited for 10 minutes, maybe 30, maybe an hour. Time had no relevance out in the wilderness. It felt as if we were living in a different world. Four days' walk from here, where the road started, was the beginning of the human world, and here in the deserted mountains was the wilderness. The two did not seem to be connected.

There was no clock here. There was nothing to indicate the days of the week. There was only a natural pattern, days lengthening and seasons changing. There was nobody counting minutes, measuring time, comparing one with the other and who created a progressing future in which things were supposed to be better than now.

Two paradise ducks flew into the valley with much commotion. Why were they calling out? I wondered. What had they seen and why were they disturbed? Were they being chased away by another animal?

I kept very still, and at first they did not see me. But when I leaned over to watch them, the branch on which I sat moved, and it wasn't long before their keen little bird eyes spotted me, and the male began to sing a warning call again. I didn't want the birds telling everyone there was a danger in this valley.

"Don't worry," I called back in bird language, imitating the consoling female call. After a few of my "hmm, hmm" the female joined me, and the male paradise duck stopped calling.

It was silent for a while. I closed my eyes. I waited. Time seemed to stop altogether.

Then finally I heard something in the distance. "Mehehehehe!" My heart missed a beat. Where was this small goat? I held my breath and waited for a second call. Upriver or up a side branch? I climbed down the tree as quickly as I could and ran over the rock face to the river. I stood still to listen again.

Nothing came. "Mehehehehe," I bleated, imitating the mother goat. Let me know where you are, I thought.

The mother had obviously walked a little way away from her young one, who was bleating to find her. They were separated long enough for me to hear in which direction they were roaming.

I climbed up the bank and struggled through the forest. The wind had brought down many trees, and I had to climb over and under big logs. I was careful not to hurt myself in my haste. The bleating appeared closer and closer, and my heart was in my throat. When I was around 20 metres (65 feet) away from the animals, I began to move very silently. I knew which branches would break, and my feet found stones to step on. Then, through the vegetation, I could see some goats climbing up a side stream. One billy was on the big rock, and three nannies and four kids were in the grass near the water.

I squatted down. My hands were shaking while I nervously took an arrow out of my quiver. I clicked an arrow onto the string.

I exhaled and I felt calm. I decided on the small billy goat that was closest to me. I drew the bow and let it go in one movement. The arrow flew straight and fast into the heart of the young goat. When he fell to the ground, the others ran into the thicket.

With adrenaline racing through my body, I ran to the dying goat. Young animals know when to give up and soon the life ebbed out of him. He was black and white, with a little brown colouring on his back. His eyes were blue.

I stroked the little creature and felt sorry for taking his life. His coat was healthy and shiny, and for a moment he felt like a little pet goat that I would carry home. But alas, we were in the wild, and we were surviving off the meat of dead animals.

I picked him up and draped him carefully over my shoulders.

He was soft and innocent. But this was the law of nature. Living and dying is the cycle of the universe. With life comes death, and with death comes life. I, too, was innocent.

We had food now, and our bodies would become stronger and healthier. Because he died, we survived.

Hunting, taking lives, even eating meat was foreign to me, for I had grown up as a vegetarian in the Netherlands. But life in the wilderness was so utterly different that I felt disconnected from my former self. I felt as if I had become another person in the mountains.

With the goat on my neck, I began to walk back to camp. The load slowed me down and it took almost two hours to get back. I had to find my way around big boulders, climb rapids, scale riverbanks, and step gingerly through swampland. My right hand was stabilizing the goat around my neck while my left hand was holding the bow. The going was slow and arduous. But with each step I felt part of the goat and his life in the forest, and therefore part of the ancient cycle of life and death.

Slowly my sadness at killing an animal turned into pride and happiness. When I came closer to our camp, I saw Peter standing on a rock. I saw the smoke of our campfire behind him in the forest. He had intuitively felt my homecoming and was looking out for me. When he saw me, he threw his arms in the air. "A goat!" he called, and I could hear the joy in his voice.

Peter took my bow, and while we walked to camp I told him where I had been and where I had seen the goats. I was always happy to see Peter. I was content to roam the forest by myself, but it was good to share beautiful times and difficult times with him – amid this vast landscape. We both loved this life.

Peter was a man who was looking for the edge: the edge of the mountains, the edge between life and death, and the edge between order and chaos. Most of all, he wanted adventure in his life. And so did I. This life was hard, tough and extreme, but also full of wonder and intensity. I always felt very alive.

With the aid of a piece of string, I hung the goat upside

down in a tree. With my hunting knife, I made small incisions. Then I peeled off his skin, cut open the stomach, and took out all the organs. With my arms full of smelly intestines, I walked to an open spot to lay down the share for the eagles. It never took very long before a bird of prey would spot me. From faraway in the sky, they kept an eye on me, for they knew I could provide the food they were after. I placed the intestines on a big boulder, and within an hour everything would be gone. In the wild nothing goes to waste.

I tied the skin of the goat to a wooden frame. Later I would try tanning it, and it would become part of a blanket. I gave Peter the heart, lungs, kidneys and liver. He would fry them on the fire and it would be the first thing we would eat. Most of the meat we would keep for the next few days. Peter would make at least three or four meals out of it.

The bones were always cooked in the same pot. After boiling everything for a long time, we would crack open the bones to get to the healthy marrow. Collagen, cartilage, gelatin, blood and fat would provide nutritional value to keep us healthy. Every organ was eaten.

In the beginning it had felt uncomfortable to murder an innocent animal for our benefit. It felt horrible, evil even. But after some time in the wilderness we connected with our instincts. The further we were away from society, the less those unwritten rules had a grip. The more our conditioning and programming waned, the more our natural instincts strengthened. Our bodies knew when to go to sleep, when to wake up, when to eat, when to go fast, when to go slowly, when to do something and when to do nothing. Our instincts would tell us where the animals were to hunt, and which one to shoot. Instinct told us to be alert – rather than afraid – when danger was lurking.

Naturally, all living creatures want to be free to roam the forest, the mountains and the valleys. Free of restrictions, free of nonsensical and illogical rules, free of conflict and free of complications. Over the years I have wondered what we are – are we humans different from other animals? What do other animals think when they see us? A walking ape with funny skin and a strong smoky smell? What is the difference between human apes and other animals? Perhaps the only difference is that we lost our natural instincts and animals never did.

While Peter was cutting up the meat, I walked to the stream to wash. The clear water was flowing endlessly from its source. It seemed to murmur a certain tune. I sang its little song while finding my way over the slippery rocks to the water. I looked at my hands that were covered in dried-up blood. I felt savage. My feet in my sandals were muddy. My T-shirt was covered in stains. I washed my hands, then undressed. Using a bar of soap, I washed my body thoroughly. Then I washed my bloody T-shirt and underwear. I rinsed my sandals and put them back on.

When I arrived at the tent, I was dry enough to put on clean and warm clothes. No hot shower for us, no bathroom, no washing machine or dryer, not even a clothes line. None of what people call "modern conveniences".

I once read an article about the Inuit. "Come to me if you need something," a grandmother had said to her grandchildren. "And I will tell you how to live without it." Life had become simple without a mortgaged house, expensive furniture, addictive technology, noisy machines and cars, and all the complexities that come with modern living. Yet the simplest life seemed the most difficult. How come other animals seem to survive so easily, yet we "clever" Homo sapiens find it so difficult to live in the wild? Other animals can fend for themselves; they can eat plants, they have thick skin, and they can handle cold and rain. Of all creatures, we seem to be the most ill-equipped.

With my long trousers and long-sleeved shirt on, I sat down on my stone around the fire. It was now past the equinox and the days were slowly drawing in. In the high mountains autumn was already encroaching. Spiderwebs were more visible and some shady places were no longer visited by the sun. Parts of the forest were now very damp. The nights were becoming cooler, and the first deer were calling out. Stags were looking for each other to fight. Every year had its cycle, and everything would forever return. Everything is part of a bigger cycle in time. Stags call, then fight, and mating follows. Then come the fawns. The young are raised and eventually they mature and go their own way. Awareness of the natural cycles gave me a sense of security and stability.

Peter cut up the liver into small strips and fried them in a pan over the fire. Then he added the kidneys and eventually the heart. The Maori of New Zealand traditionally believed that by eating the heart you would receive the "mana", which was the power and spiritual essence of the animal or human. I could now see why they believed that. After hunting and eating the animal, I felt more and more like that wild creature. I began to feel more quiet, balanced and strong.

After we had eaten the organs, the fire was getting low. But the sun was still above the mountains.

"What do you think, is there still time to explore?" said Peter.

I jumped up and grabbed two walking sticks. "Which way?" I said eagerly.

Peter looked around. The wind had picked up again. He turned his back to the wind.

"We haven't looked yet at that big overhanging rock face over there," he said. "Who knows what we will find."

"Moa bones?" I joked. "A goat house? A cave?"

"Dry firewood, if nothing else," said Peter. And we set off in a westerly direction.

We were in the middle of a vast wilderness. It was quite likely no human had ever set foot here. There were no trails, except for animal tracks. Our eyes were trained in finding those pathways, and slowly we climbed up the side of the mountain. But it was steeper than we had anticipated. Sometimes we had to pull ourselves up onto small trees. Rocks were loose and crumbling under our feet. We had to focus to prevent ourselves from falling. It required attention – there was no space or time to be distracted.

Eventually we came out at the rock face. It was dry at the bottom because the gigantic limestone was shaped in such a way that it had become a little roof. The sand had never been wet, and it was clear that the goats had discovered this spot, too, because there were many droppings. On the side of the rock, we saw beautiful mosses. They were clinging onto the rocks with hardly any soil. We observed tiny little star flowers in the moss. They were so delicate yet they were able to survive in the high mountains. It was the most beautiful little garden.

While we were looking around, a native robin turned up – a grey little bird with long stick legs. Rather than flying toward us, he seemed to drop down from the sky. He looked curiously at us. It was perhaps the first time he had seen apes in this spot. He hopped closer, and eventually landed on my sandal. Peter and I slowly sat down on a rock. Like most native birds, the little robin was not scared and was determined to investigate us further. He flew to the tree, and a second later landed on Peter's head. He pecked at his hair and hopped around for a while. After some more fluttering about, he eventually left us.

"Bye, bye, little robin," said Peter with a smile.

Then the robin began to sing from a tree not far from us. The sound reflected off the rock face and was so piercing that it hurt our ears.

"Aha, you are the emperor of this valley!" I said with a laugh.

"We will call you an imperial bird!" said Peter.

We sat down on the yellow-coloured limestone.

"Shall we move our camp up and sleep here?" I asked with a laugh. "Wouldn't it be cool to stay in this place?" I had always dreamed of living in a cave. But all the caves we had found were either wet or almost impossible to reach.

After fantasizing where to make our beds, and how to dig tables and chairs out of the soft sandstone, we reluctantly stood up and returned to camp. On the way we found an old, dead fallen tree. The roots were exposed, and we managed to break some off. Roots were the best firewood.

We reached the tent as the sun was setting. I took my dry clothes from the manuka bushes and picked some branches for tea. The tea-tree shrub contained vitamin C and it made a nice herbal tea.

Peter had rekindled the fire, gathered water from the river in the billy pot and placed it onto the hook. With three sticks and some rope, I had knotted a tripod. With a length of rope I had attached an iron hook from a piece of wire. It was the perfect cooking implement. If the fire was fierce, we could lift the three sticks up, and if it was very low, we could lower the whole set down.

I sat down and looked at the flames while Peter was studying the map.

"We were here today," he said, and pointed at the symbols that indicated a high cliff. "Interesting, had we gone up higher, we could have seen a little pond. There must have been a spring not far from there."

"Really?" I said, envisioning staying in the cave since there was drinking water nearby. "We should go there."

"Have you forgotten what a hellish journey it was to get there?" laughed Peter. "Imagine that with a 25-kilo [55-pound] backpack, your bow in one hand and the camp oven in the other."

"I will walk twice! Three times!" I said with a grin, but I knew it would be an unlikely event. Moving camp was no easy matter.

We listened to the silence. There was not a sigh of wind, only a bellbird in the far distance. Then I felt a slight inner disturbance. A few seconds later my brain registered an engine. An aeroplane was flying over. I wondered who was inside. People who were looking at the in-flight magazine, sipping coffee, looking at their phones, trying to sleep. Maybe one or two were looking out of the window. They would see nothing but snow-capped mountains, a vast trackless wilderness. Would they ever consider somebody was down there, looking up at them? Two little creatures around a fire, looking at the plane from another world?

Would they ever guess we had not seen another human for

many weeks? Could they imagine that in the last few years we had become closer to animals than to our own species? That we were in tune with nature, with our senses and our natural instincts?

Would they know that it is possible to live in the wild, the way our nomadic ancestors did? What would they do, I wondered, if their aeroplane dropped down from the sky? Would they know how to light a fire, how to build a shelter to stay warm? Would they feel at home on the earth they were born on?

"Could you eat more meat today?" asked Peter.

"I am almost full but I think I could eat more," I said, and I stood up to get it. The more we could eat, the less would go rotten. Peter had hung the meat in a tree above the creek where it was cooler. He had covered it in a muslin cloth to stop the blowflies laying eggs. I carefully untied the fabric, and with my sharp hunter's knife I cut out the back steaks, the tenderest part of the animal.

"The frying pan is hot," said Peter as he put a spoonful of fat in it. After we had killed a deer a month ago, we had rendered down the fat and saved it in a jar. Now we cooked everything in venison fat, which was very tasty.

I cut off two slices of camp-oven bread that we had baked some days before and placed it in the frying pan. When they were nicely browned, Peter put in the meat. It did not take very long before the bread and steaks were ready to eat. We took a piece of toast with the meat and chewed it slowly. We stared at the fire. When all the food was gone, we took a little stick from a nearby branch to clean our teeth.

The sun was setting behind us, casting a red glow over the entire horizon. The big white stones in the riverbed looked a little more yellow, a nearby rock face had an orange glow, and little purple flowers were slowly closing their petals for the night.

Peter's face looked warm and beautiful. When I caught his eyes, I saw they were shining.

"Nice, isn't it?" he said softly.

"Yes." I smiled. I felt very happy.

Everything was more intense in the mountains: hunger, thirst, heat, freezing cold, tremendous storms. And happiness. There was no greater sense of contentment and feeling of being connected to everything than in the wilderness.

Dusk was gathering and birds began to sing their evening chorus. Daylight was slowly withdrawing from the forest. Darkness encroached and a cool breeze picked up. We moved a little closer to the flames.

"How many years have humans sat like this around the fire?" said Peter.

"Millions," I answered. "Our brain understands fire very well. Also rivers, mountains and forests."

"Our ancestors survived living like this for centuries," he said. "At school they tell us that we survived by staying safe. But I think we survived by being courageous. Imagine how brave you had to be to kill a mammoth. They were risking their lives. Now we are encouraged to stay safe and secure. But that mentality will be our downfall in the end. It is not the principle on which we survived all those years."

"How should humans live instead, do you think?" I asked.

"Dangerously," he said with a laugh. "Take risks all the time – not risking your life in a physical sense but taking psychological risks. Live on the edge without security. Venture into the unknown. Which means you should not listen to all of your cultural conditioning. Others will tell you what you are supposed to do, what is supposed to be good for you, which way you are supposed to be living, what you are supposed to be thinking. I am not saying do the opposite of what they tell you, but to simply question it. Do you really need a job in order to live? Do you have to earn to support your life, or is living quite enough?"

"Well, yeah, you need money," I said, as a matter of fact.

"Yes, I think it's important to figure out what money symbolizes. Money represents your time. Your life is basically a limited period of time. So you have to be very careful how you spend it. Therefore, you have to be careful with money. The more money you waste, the more time you will have to work. It is great if you love your job, but a lot of people would rather be doing something else."

A little robin began to sing his loud song. He was not far away, and his voice was again very piercing.

"The imperial bird is speaking," I laughed.

It was dark now, and although we weren't tired, we were getting colder and were ready to go into the tent.

"Let's go to bed," I said, while searching for our toothbrushes.

Peter collected a little ash from the fire. Within a second his teeth looked pitch-black. We first brushed our teeth with ash, then we used toothpaste to turn them white again.

We crawled underneath our opossum skins and felt warm. It was a beautiful, still night so we left the tent door open. The air was nice and fresh. Through the branches, I looked up at the night sky and saw many stars.

An owl called out. In the distance, another morepork answered.

"How could anyone feel alone in the wilderness?" said Peter. "There are animals all around us."

An opossum called out. "Ch-ch-ch-ch-ch." We waited for another to bark back, but nothing came. It was silent again.

"And even if there are no animals, then there are flowers, plants and trees," I said.

"And even if you are in a sandy desert," said Peter, "there is a sun, moon, many stars and galaxies."

"One thing is for certain," I said, "you are never really alone. You just have to think bigger."

And with that thought I felt my eyes become heavy and moments of the day flash by. The rising sun, flowing river, all the sounds, green leaves in the wind, a moving kaleidoscope, my little goat around my neck, the cave, dancing flames of the fire, and the stars above me.

Everything today had been pure, peaceful and innocent.

BECOMING ANIMAL

Owning up to being an animal, a creature of earth. Tuning our animal senses to the sensible terrain: blending our skin with the rain-rippled surface of rivers, mingling our ears with the thunder and the thrumming of frogs, and our eyes with the molten sky. Feeling the polyrhythmic pulse of this place – this huge windswept body of water and stone. This vexed being in whose flesh we're entangled.

Becoming earth. Becoming animal. Becoming, in this manner, fully human.

From *Becoming Animal* by David Abram, Pantheon, 2010. Permission granted by David Abram.

David is an eco-philosopher and writer from New York, well known for coining the term 'more-than-human world'. He is also the founder and creative director of the Alliance for Wild Ethics, a collaboration of organizations aiming to help us collectively shift to a more eco-centred culture.

After six years with the US army and nearly five years as a consultant with McKinsey & Company, Sophie exited the rat race and embarked on a solo journey of self-discovery. Currently a student of nature, she explores the USA and Mexico by van and teaches herself practical self-reliance. Sophie homesteads on 41 hectares (102 acres) in Kentucky, where she is building a tiny off-grid home and working toward her goal of living completely off the land.

This is what moved her during her expedition to the summit of Mount Everest.

WAKING UP ON EVEREST

SOPHIE SUNG-BIN HILAIRE

Apparently, seeing three recently deceased bodies near Everest's summit is uncommon. All we could do was silently pray for their souls. Rescue helicopters couldn't reach us at that altitude, and there were limited options for a safe ground rescue.

Someone later said the first body we passed still appeared to be breathing. I didn't recall a hand being exposed on the way up, but on the way down a glove was off, which didn't make sense since it was minus 40 degrees. I had heard stories of people losing their minds up here and tearing their layers off, thinking they were overheating — and subsequently freezing to death. My oxygen mask concealed the crestfallen expression on my face. Agony washed over me in waves as I watched hypoxia unfold in real time.

I silently recalled there have been over 300 recorded deaths on Everest.

Tears quietly filled my oxygen mask as my crampons rhythmically crunched into the ice, past the three bodies. Just like I wept when I was startled by the first dead body we encountered a couple of days earlier, hanging like a grim scarecrow on the steep, icy mountainside. The body hung only a few feet away from a tent of Lhotse climbers at Camp 3. I could only assume it was their former teammate.

The dead were left out on display, close to camp, while teams waited to hear back from the deceased climbers' families regarding wishes for their disposal. It is difficult enough to exist on Everest, but even harder to climb while moving extra weight.

Ultimately, the stiffened bodies are either left in place to become frozen landmarks, cut free to slide deep into a crevasse, or unceremoniously dragged for days back down to base camp to fly back to family – for a small fortune.

"If you can move, GET DOWN! Don't be another dead body people have to climb over!" I heard a man yelling at a fellow climber who was seated in front of him.

Never sit down, I remembered hearing from Ang Dorjee, my guide. *When climbers sit down, they never get back up*. I was jolted back to my current reality, approaching the 8,000-metre (26,247-foot) elevation "Death Zone" where the human body breaks down at an accelerated rate. The objective is to spend as little time there as possible. The sound of someone yelling hung strangely in the atmosphere, as most people were conserving every ounce of energy for the final push of this climb that most had spent years preparing for.

As I lifted my boot to take another step, I was startled by something pulling back. I looked down and saw my crampon caught on the line. My brows furrowed in frustration as I began to track the line to its source. Suddenly I was the one ready to yell at another climber for sitting down and endangering the rest of us. But once I illuminated the full section of line with my headlamp, my face softened. They wouldn't have heard me if I'd yelled.

It was someone who had sat down and never got back up.

As the figure and I briefly connected through the tension of the rope, we became one for a split second. I felt the weight of their frozen, heavy heart.

A moment of reality set in. Thoughts of self-doubt began to repeat … thoughts about how no one actually needs to summit Mount Everest.

We find the conviction to climb for the reasons we tell ourselves. However, witnessing the amount of death from this voluntary experience caused me to ask some involuntary questions.

Did the dead climber and I share a moment at base camp?

What were they searching for?

Did they find it?

I winced. One step at a time, I continued my laboured footsteps up the mountain. How could I not question my own health and sanity as I moved through the carnage in the darkness?

Did they know they were dying?

Did it happen suddenly?

As their life slipped away, did they regret their decision to climb to the top of the world?

And what about me? I was certainly nauseous and dry-heaving from the altitude. Despite being on oxygen, I was still gasping for air at times.

Was I about to take my final step?

Why does Mother Nature allow some of us to pass through inhospitable conditions, but keeps others for her collection of frozen bodies?

What the hell am I doing up here?

With death surrounding me as I climbed through the night, it was difficult to summon excitement for the moment I'd been imagining for years.

It seemed so much better in my dreams.

———————

How did I end up in such a place?

To be honest, I didn't know life without danger. It started in my childhood, which could have easily been a horror movie given the blood, violence and chainsaws involved.

It wasn't just my own memories – humans carry 14 generations of ancestral trauma in our DNA through epigenetic inheritance, and there were dark pasts on both sides of my family that I was only partially aware of. Most of the harrowing stories were buried with time. I'll never be able to tell them, but my cells remember.

It's highly probable that no one in my lineage was even

aware they had a choice in working through their shadows and transmuting them into light. For no fault of their own, they lacked access to knowledge and resources. Most of them struggled through life the best they knew how, unconsciously handing off a variant of the cycle of abuse to the next generation. I have found that such cycles are universal to the human experience, and unfortunately not unique to my story.

At the age of 17, I decided to attend college at West Point, a taxpayer-funded full ride that came with a five-year army commitment, which I ultimately extended to six years. A few years earlier 9/11 had happened, and going to war in the Middle East was a guarantee that I, quite honestly, looked forward to.

For better or worse, I'm atypically calm around violence. While friends routinely told me they could not imagine joining the army, I felt a calling: it felt exciting and important.

Extreme physical exertion was my socially acceptable method of playing with the demons that were passed on to me. Previous attempts to escape the discomfort deep in my psyche – including alcohol abuse and a long list of other reckless behaviours – had left me with unsavoury consequences. Arrests, hospitalizations, a stint at a halfway home ... my personal life was in stark contrast to my stellar academic record. I had to find another outlet.

Chasing endorphins through exercise started at West Point, where I enrolled as one of the least athletic cadets in my class. It was there that I started training for marathons and would eventually earn the Guinness World Record for the Fastest Marathon in Full Military Uniform. I felt I had found another calling – I could leverage the tiger-parented, insecure overachiever deep within me to achieve feats that inspired others.

At that age, I was not aware that healing the root cause of my suffering was a possibility. No wise adults in my life had ever explained what that even meant. But something was different for me than it was for any of my ancestors: I was born into financial privilege to an upper middle-class family in Ohio.

What's more, I was uniquely designed as an empath – someone

who feels the emotions of others. This gift gave me a generous dose of empathy for those who violated and unconsciously projected their darkness on me throughout the years.

Even without a roadmap on where to go or how to heal myself, I was always pushing myself beyond my perceived limits and questioning the status quo. The black sheep no matter where I went, I loved challenging people's perceptions by rebelling against choice societal norms. But deep down I knew I was holding on to other self-sabotaging patterns. And unfortunately only rebelling against myself.

———————————

The Tibetan name for Everest is Chomolungma, which translates to "Goddess Mother of Mountains". Over 99 per cent of climbers use oxygen and take two full months to summit and descend. The typical season runs from 1 April through 31 May.

Climbers must purchase permits, which only allow for summit attempts during a predetermined two-week window. The window coincides with the best historical chance of summiting with regards to weather – but does not guarantee favourable conditions.

To naturally increase red blood-cell count for altitude acclimatization, climbers will "climb high, sleep low". In other words, most climbers will ascend partway up the mountain, then descend back down to base camp, twice. Then, they will make their third and final push from base camp, past all four camps, to the summit.

Climbing Everest was different from the other dangerous arenas I knew. Being in peak physical condition was a critical element for getting to the starting line, but ultimately could have zero impact on the result.

I was not in charge, Mother Nature was.

Whiteouts, avalanches, unexpected heart problems at never-before-tested elevations for the body I had spent 31 years in – it was all fair game in this precarious dance with the most powerful forces on earth.

Through numerous modalities, I cultivated a strong mindset that would push beyond levels of discomfort I had never felt. But I had to be meticulous about not pushing an ounce beyond that, into my own injury or death.

Ego exists in all human beings but is undeniably pronounced in each year's group of Everest climbers. Understanding whether one's ego sits more on the side of impressing others versus pushing the boundaries of one's own perceived limits, is a question each climber must uncover on their own.

Personally, both sides had been part of my life journey. But regardless of the reason, I was looking forward to the outdoor adventure and associated adrenaline I lacked in my corporate career. It was such a welcome thrill for me that I decided to invest extraordinary amounts of time and money into pursuing the dream.

Could I make it to the top of planet earth?

And if I did, what wisdom from the universe would I bring back to sea level?

Knowing I could not control the expedition's outcome based on a myriad of external circumstances, I boarded my flight to Kathmandu with a single objective: to return from two months in nature as a wiser, more evolved version of myself.

As I've grown, I've realized that Mother Nature is always speaking to us. Usually softly, though sometimes she roars. I longed to be the type of person who could predict the next hour's weather from her faint whispers, but the truth was I had squandered many years looking at screens instead of the sky.

For climbers who have not spent the requisite time in nature to become fluent in her language, "translators" in the form of Sherpas and guides, are necessary for survival. According to our guides, this year's two-week summit window was not going to be a generous one. Adventure Consultants had pioneered commercialized climbing on Everest in the 1990s; I felt safe in the hands of their experienced guides and Sherpas. Rarely did they miss the summit window entirely. They paid handsomely for a select Swiss weather forecasting service, which was as reliable as forecasts could be on Everest. But even that fluctuated daily.

Avalanches became increasingly frequent as the weather warmed throughout the summer. Whenever one struck while we were "safe" at base camp, I would turn immediately to Ang Dorjee. Usually he would wink and say with confidence, "No worry, chicken curry." He and his ancestors were spiritually connected to the Himalayas; there was an undeniable wisdom that surrounded him like an aura. But when we heard or saw avalanches while climbing, we would stop in our tracks and wait for him to finish a prayer while tossing a rice offering to the gods.

We climbers think we are powerful, but we are merely fragile ants who could be swallowed whole at any moment by a crevasse, the endless voids we peeked at while crossing over rickety horizontal ladders. Observing Ang Dorjee's spiritual practices helped me acknowledge and connect to the magnificence of the nature that surrounded us, transcending beyond our tiny bodies into something divine.

22 May 2019: Weather forecast
Extremely tricky. Be vigilant. It is deadly.
−33°C (−28°F), −45°C (−50°F) with windchill

Our summit push started at 10pm from Camp 4. I had tried to nap for a few hours in my sleeping bag, but my nerves had got the better of me. As I layered on my gear, I teetered on the edge of dread and excitement for the impending moment where I would step out of the tent and into the frigid night air. I inhaled a deep breath of rubber-flavoured oxygen as I mentally transitioned into the most perilous part of the journey.

Once I emerged from my tent, I heard murmurings from the other teams and saw puffs of breath among the scattered headlamps. I had no concept of where the summit was, but I could make out a trail of headlamps in the distance from teams who had already set off. I wondered what was going through their minds.

It was the slowest I had seen climbers moving on the mountain.

Every day on the mountain had felt like "go time", but today was the one that everything had led up to. I knew this in my mind but struggled to attach it to an embodied thrill in my stomach and heart. I didn't feel strong, but at least I wasn't depleted.

I focused on the spotlight directly in front of my heavy footsteps in order to distract myself from my altitude-induced nausea. Every so often, I would glance up into the darkness at the strand of vibrating headlamps. But without being able to see the summit, the view was demoralizing, and I immediately regretted looking.

I came to an ice wall that the climbers ahead were struggling with. There is a fixed line that runs all the way from base camp to the summit of Everest, which is emplaced by a highly skilled team of Sherpas called the Icefall Doctors. They also repair the route as often as possible. Sections of the Khumbu Ice Fall shift several metres daily – revealing massive crevasses – and avalanches can make a section impassible within seconds.

It is unsafe for a climber to unclip from the fixed line for any reason other than to move around an anchor point, and rare for a Sherpa or guide to ask a climber to do so. But as we approached the wall of exhausted climbers, Ang Dorjee and Rinji, my Sherpa, motioned for me to follow them. We unclipped and moved at a brisk pace, creating our own path through thigh-deep snow, sometimes on all fours, untethered from the mountain.

Is this what a heart attack feels like?

I was well-versed with pushing myself to cardio failure, but this was a different beast. I was not in control and had no concept of where or when we would catch a break. I trusted Ang Dorjee and Rinji and kept up – gulping air through my oxygen mask, lungs on fire, down suit soaked with sweat, no longer aware of my nausea. On plenty of other mountains, this would have been a leisurely trot. Up in the Death Zone with only one-third of the oxygen we relish at sea level, I sensed myself creeping toward the edge of my limits.

After what felt like an eternity, we passed the pile-up and slowed back down to our normal pace. Ang Dorjee explained we needed to pass them in order to reduce our time in the Death

Zone. The other climbers were moving too slowly. I was grateful to my body for not collapsing, and grateful to Ang Dorjee for his decades of wisdom on this mountain.

Eight hours went by like this – trudging upward in the dark, no view of the summit, minimal breaks, scanning my body to make sure I was not on the verge of succumbing to frostbite. I stayed connected to my body via the sound of my breath through my mask and the thud of my heart beating out of my chest. Occasionally I would realize the magnality of the moment I was living in, and a tear of gratitude would roll into my oxygen mask. No part of me was thinking about my life back in Manhattan.

Despite the exhaustion, every cell in my being was buzzing with something acutely primal, the rawness of my human existence.

Was my vision acting up, or was the sky actually turning into a sparkling sapphire?

I began to see features beyond my 1-metre diameter headlamp spotlight. The backdrop faded into lapis, then took on an amethyst hue. Ahead of me I still could not see the summit … but I did see climbers disappearing behind a mound.

And suddenly I recognized the scene before me, as I had seen it in many photos when I used to daydream of this moment. I had dared not to fantasize about this view throughout the expedition, but suddenly it was happening before my eyes and in my body: I was approaching the summit of Everest.

Frequently there is no view at the summit. On a cloudy day, all you will see is the snow and ice beneath your feet, and I was prepared for that reality. But today was not one of those days. We were rewarded with a spectacular landscape I will never forget.

Down to my left, I saw the first glimpse of sunlight touch the otherworldly backdrop of lavender mountains that faded into a soft haze. These were some of the highest peaks in the world, several of them also over 8,000 metres (26,247 feet) tall: Lhotse, Cho Oyu and Makalu. I realized that I was looking *down* at them. The corners of my mouth behind my oxygen mask unconsciously curled upward. I had experienced similar views while flying in planes, but this time my feet were firmly planted on the ground. Who was to say if I was still in Nepal, or technically in Tibet?

Suddenly, a sparkling feeling enveloped my body like a scene out of a cartoon – I have no way of describing it other than I had everything I ever wanted in life. My feet were rooted in the earth, my soul was floating in heaven. Those final steps to the peak felt like a gentle dream.

While standing on a point on the planet that many would perceive as the pinnacle of ego, I no longer existed. I was so immersed in the energy around me that my ego completely dissolved. Had the thought even crossed my mind, the notion of "conquering" nature would have been absurd – I had stepped into nature, really entered her. This fragile ant became one with nature's grandeur.

For the first time in my life, I was whole.

With my oxygen mask still on, my wonderstruck expression was a secret to those around me. I recalled the accounts I had read of others' moments on this very summit, many of them admittedly unable to fully take it in, emotionally numb until they returned to a lower elevation due to utter fatigue. I saw that numbness in a pair of glazed eyes with frozen eyelashes that trudged past me. I recognized and congratulated the climber as he vacantly moved onward like a ghost. I was probably a ghost to him, too.

After 20-some minutes of euphoria, Ang Dorjee and Rinji motioned for us to begin our descent. With each step, I painfully felt the distance increase between me and the summit. All I wanted to do was turn around and go back up. The magnetism of the summit's pull was unquestionable.

Nothing else mattered. The chains had vanished. I was free. It felt like Home in a way I had never known.

Descending to Camp 4 took twice as long as the route up. Most climbing accidents occur on the way down, as climbers are hyper-fixated on the summit and rationing adrenaline isn't top of their minds. A mix of emotions swept through me on the way down: heartbreak for the increasing distance between myself and heaven with each backward glance, but gratitude for the invaluable inner shift I had come here for.

I genuinely wondered, Will I ever feel that sense of wholeness and freedom again?

Back at Camp 4 I took a nap, ecstasy still coursing through my veins. When I woke up, I felt elation for the accomplishment of a decade-long goal – quickly followed by despair for how much my spirit missed Home. But my mind rapidly detached from the real-life dream I had just experienced and returned to the realities of the expedition. My next mission was to safely descend back to base camp over the following week. Of the five climbers on our team, three had not been able to complete the expedition due to cerebral oedema, pneumonia and frostbite. Fortunately all of them would survive without injuries.

I shifted back into mission mode and saved the deep thoughts for later.

—————————

Everest made me feel alive in a way I could never match in the society I'd unconsciously subscribed to. When I returned to Manhattan, I was no longer the same burned-out consultant who had packed her expedition duffels and set off for a dream.

In her place was a woman who steeped herself in nature to reconnect with her innate wildness. A woman who faced the delicate reality of her human experience and was granted safe passage. She was decidedly not the same – and could never go back – because she had a new barometer for what being alive meant.

My spirit was now consumed by the harsh dissonance between my new-found perspective from the wild and my reality as an obedient slave to society. I could no longer overlook the wiser, freer version of myself, suffocating underneath the blanket of misery my ancestors had clutched onto for centuries.

Returning to work with my laptop of anxiety-inducing emails – all while wearing an overpriced, uncomfortable suit – felt utterly pointless.

But the darkest moments were when I went to sleep, no longer able to distract myself with the chaos and meaningless tasks that filled my days. My inner voice screamed at my ego to set myself free. Wise enough to know better, but still not brave enough to exit the matrix, I willingly put my shackles back on and re-entered society … but this time, as an insomniac.

Mercifully, nature's medicine was already in my veins and she continued to purify me, so long as I kept taking steps toward a more intentional life. Over the next few years, I embraced and embodied my rebellious nature for good. For as Nietzsche said, "We have to be careful that in throwing out the devil, we don't throw out the best part of ourselves." At last I began to shed the layers of societal pressure that the generations before me had felt obligated to.

Longstanding, toxic relationships were released with a sigh of relief. The Manhattan apartment that couldn't see the sky became vacant. And finally, with much jubilation, I stepped into pure self-integrity by resigning from my unfulfilling career.

My daily surroundings became nature-filled when I moved into a Sprinter van named Sage for the price of six months' rent in my old apartment. I spent nearly all my time in solitude, re-evaluating my values without the influence of a community.

With my renewed perspective of who I am and why I am here, memories bubbled to the surface that I had buried throughout my lifetime, and many lifetimes before. I forgave myself for the years of self-abandonment I'd committed until I escaped the environments that clouded my judgement in the first place.

I had outsourced all my power: looking to authority figures for guidance, to experts for answers, to mentors for blueprints – when all along, I had the answers inside of me. Turns out I just had to get away from humankind's clever distractions to hear the whispers of my own soul.

There were specific moments that unquestionably levelled me up on my spiritual awakening.

A solo journey into Montana's wilderness cured my insomnia …

when a primordial scream released a weighty generational curse.

A visit to a popular healing centre turned out to be a heavily commoditized disappointment ... when viewed through my eyes that were attuned to the natural world.

A hike in Colorado taught me that I could connect with nature just as profoundly as I had on Everest ... for far less money and training.

No longer accepting others' projections as my own reality, I took the pen and became the author of my story. With surprising ease I discarded the barriers to the truth that had been passed down through my lineage. I moved onto a 41-hectare (102-acre) homestead in Kentucky and began a new life of self-reliance in nature, giving my love and energy that had once gone into PowerPoint, directly into my land. And I fully receive nature's love in reciprocation.

My years of solitude with Sage were critical for me to hear and nurture my own inner voice, but my new azimuth would eventually lead me toward an aligned community of off-grid enthusiasts who matched my frequency. For us feral creatures, time is no longer on a Monday through Friday, nine-to-five schedule. Monday may as well be Saturday. Through purpose-driven action, we have taken back our time. Each day is limitless and spent doing what truly matters. We are free.

Everest gave me the ultimate gift: a higher perspective that forced me to take action to free myself. What could have become just another accomplishment to toss in the bottomless void of feats for conditional love, materialized into thoughtful steps to fill that void with self-love. Just as I surrendered to the power of nature on Everest, I surrendered to my true nature and incarnated the powerful woman my younger self did not dare to dream of becoming. I "pretired" at 34 and vowed to spend the rest of my life in discovery.

What better way to honour my ancestors' longings and unfinished business than to recalibrate the DNA further from the diseases that plagued us? It's the least I can do for the unconditional love they embraced me with on the top of the world. Breaking the chains of addiction, violence and other inherited limiting beliefs means I'm not the only one who gets to enjoy this bliss: each of us has the power to make an anthropological imprint on the collective psyche. And if a family is in my future, our lineage will evolve for 14 generations to come.

To live an extraordinary life one must be willing to face extraordinary challenges. Admittedly I was once furious about the cards I was dealt. Now I honestly could not be more grateful – the strongest steel is forged by the hottest fire. The rewards on the other side have been unparalleled: the gratification of growth, the serenity of self-acceptance and the fulfillment of discovering my purpose.

I smile, knowing the lessons from my personal mountain range are what will enable me to summit the inevitable peaks that lie ahead. And so I bow in gratitude to every peak and valley along my path.

Namaste.

————————

You cannot stay on the summit forever; you have to come down again. So why bother in the first place?

Just this: what is above knows what is below, but what is below does not know what is above.

One climbs, one sees. One descends, one sees no longer, but one has seen.

There is an art of conducting oneself in the lower regions by the memory of what one saw higher up.

When one can no longer see, one can at least still know.

From *Mount Analogue* by René Daumal, Vincent Stuart Ltd., 1959.

THE JOURNEY

BY DAVID WHYTE

Above the mountains
the geese turn into
the light again

painting their
black silhouettes
on an open sky.

Sometimes everything
has to be
enscribed across
the heavens

so you can find
the one line
already written
inside you.

Sometimes it takes
a great sky

to find that
first, bright
and indescribable
wedge of freedom
in your own heart.

Sometimes with
the bones of the black
sticks left when the fire
has gone out

someone has written
something new
in the ashes
of your life.

You are not leaving.
Even as the light
fades quickly now,
you are arriving.

David is an internationally acclaimed poet,
author and speaker living in the Pacific Northwest.
He is passionate about representing the beauty
of the human experience.

Karl is a British ex-paratrooper who in 1998 initiated a challenge he named the Goliath expedition. He is hoping to become the first person to walk an unbroken path from South America to his home in the UK, unassisted by transport, walking over the ice in the Arctic and other dangerous environments.
He is still walking.

This is a story about an experience he had while walking the Darien Gap in 2001, known as one of the most dangerous places on earth – the jungle between Colombia and Panama.

BECOMING CAIMAN

KARL BUSHBY

When people talk about a unique moment in life, oddly enough I cannot help but think of … well, life, as being momentary. Life is a relatively short unique moment in space and time. A moment bookended by the celebration of birth and our fear of death. Death, our concept of death, is one of the most interesting motivators, for me at least. It's not normally part of our story, and it's not something that gets a lot of attention. Which sometimes strikes me as a little odd. In a universe dominated by probability, death appears to be the only strange exception, with a probability ratio of 100 per cent. No generalization, no fractions, no equivocations, no ifs, no buts, you die, and where the hell is the meaning and a purpose in that? You would think that would determine everything we do, but yet …

I guess my slightly darker worldview, at a seemingly young age, stems from a military career. I've buried friends in Northern Ireland and, as paratroopers, we lived knowing that our estimated life expectancy on a modern battlefield was 60 minutes.

That aside, why doesn't our mortality play a more seemingly obvious role in our lives? Aware of our own mortality, you would think all our decisions would be shaped by that single fact. I mean, think about it. I'm sure you have occasionally, but rarely if you are young. When I'm asked the question why – why journey like I do, walking around the world for over decades – this is some of the reasoning I naturally gravitate to. The problem of life, and what to do about it. Not that I'm going to always admit that.

Most of us seem to invest our time in creating strategies and ideologies that outright deny death, effectively creating our own eternal safe spaces. I systematically did away with those options by the time I was 20, leaving me with the less comfortable tick-tock of inevitability. That tends to focus you, shape your thinking, worldview and priorities. In my case it's just one of a number of factors that ultimately led to me one day standing, staring down a road some 48,000 kilometres (30,000 miles), and decades, long. Standing there, in the most distant land, with only $500 US dollars to my name and no idea how I am going to make it home. At which point you are no longer seeking adventure, it's coming for you, like storming ocean waves. And so, finally, you get your chance to rage, rage against the dying of the light. Within that, you find meaning and a purpose, and overnight you feel like you have become the richest poor man in the world. A wealth of experiences – so many it's impossible to single one out among the cacophony. Yet, among all those stories of high adventure, sometimes it's the little things and the stuff in-between that can get overlooked, that can be amazing.

Sitting in Medellin, Colombia, in November 2000, death would have been a pressing concern. After two years and thousands of miles, I had reached the last city in South America. In front of me was the first true test, and the first of three controversial gaps linking all the continents together – a 200-mile swathe of pristine trackless jungle, bordering Colombia and Panama. Also, the frontline of a decades-long war between the Revolutionary Armed Forces of Colombia (FARC) and the Colombian government. It was known as the darkest place on earth at the time. It had an impressive body count, including a number of foreigners who had been foolish enough to enter the region.

FARC was fighting the government on 60 fronts throughout the periphery of the country. I faced the 35th front: the area known as the Darien Gap, so-called as you could drive from Prudhoe Bay in Alaska down to Punta Arenas in Chile except for the Darien. There is no road through the Gap. It gets its name from the Darien National Park on the Panamanian side of the border.

This was a concern. The region was a desperate mix of insurgency, counterinsurgency, drug production, smuggling, gun-running, counter-narcotics operations being run by Colombia's drug cartels and a number of opposing forces/gangs, and agencies from the US and Colombian governments. It was an understatement to say it was confusing and complex. Overlay this with the most demanding physical terrain, and the word "challenge" seems to fall short. It begins where the Andes peter out into lowlands and the mighty Atrato River, beyond which lies hundreds of kilometres of jungle, rivers and swamps. You don't walk into the Darien, you take boats, except I can't take boats as they are classed as transport, which is not allowed under the expedition rules I made for myself.

I had to get creative. In Medellin, I spoke to anyone and everyone I could who had anything to do with the Darien region or the Colombian state of Chóco. Journalists, police, military, and anyone who had worked there, and with this information began building a picture of what was in front of me. From that, I devised a series of route options in phases to get in, through and out to Panama City. Getting into the Darien Gap was the first challenge. The remaining mountains and valleys were crossed by a single road leading north for a few hundred kilometres, dotted with a number of hotly contested small towns. These towns mark the frontline of fighting between FARC and their adversaries, the Colombian army, and a right-wing militia known as the AUC or Auto Defence Force. The AUC was a notorious right-wing death squad responsible for massacres throughout Colombia.

One day I paid a visit to the regional police headquarters, responsible for the defence of Medellin and the state of Antioquia. I was accompanied by my newly found girlfriend at the time from Medellin; we had become quite close very quickly.

Left alone while waiting for an interview with police chiefs, I decided to push my luck and stepped into an office off the corridor, as there did not seem to be anyone around. Bingo. Lining the walls were a series of maps with standard NATO military symbology denoting FARC's dispositions. In my last job in the army, I was part of the battalion's intelligence cell and maps were my business. And all of this made instant sense to me. Looking over the maps I could see where everything was – FARC units, a direction of movement, possible HQ locations – and it's where I learned the front northwest of Medellin was the 35th front, including information on the AUC. All of this was helping me to form a picture of the world in front of me. At which point someone entered the room, surprised to find me, demanding to know what I was doing there. The skinny, long-haired gringo hippy looked confused. Did I just want the bathroom? I was ushered back out into the corridor.

I came up with two route options I named the Red Route and Black Route. The latter would avoid all contact with the population. A hardcore cross-country option that would ultimately prove unfeasible as I would just not be able to realistically carry the supplies needed. Ultimately I would need to use those towns along the road north to feed off, which, as I was reminded by a military commander, would be a very real problem as anything that moves on that road is being watched by all sides. At this time Colombia was the world's "kidnap central", with many left-wing guerilla groups making money out of the kidnapping business.

The plan was to simply dumb myself down from a Western backpacker to a homeless vagrant seemingly of little worth to anyone. All you would get from me were ticks and fleas. Beyond the "road phase" I would switch to jungle mode, finding my way through the swamps to the Atrato River. Next, the river phase would require me to float for however many days it took downstream until I was within reach of firm enough ground allowing me to head into the Darien proper and for Colombia's border with Panama.

The road and the first jungle phases were scary as hell: evading FARC groups and surviving encounters with the AUC – people who would not have thought twice about killing me – keeping my wits about me, trying to avoid being eaten alive by mosquitoes and other creatures, and staying in a military camp for the latter parts while I prepared myself for the next part of my journey. It was that very next part, the river phase, that proved an eye-opener.

Jungle mode was designed specifically for escape and evasion. I worked on a layered system. First, my one layer of cloth, a heavy material meant to deal with the rough jungle environment. My shirt and trousers had been reinforced in parts and within these fabric modifications were hidden numerous items I might need to survive in worst-case scenarios. If I was captured and stripped of my equipment, left with only the clothes I stood in, within that clothing, sewn into hems and collar and between layers of material, was a number of items. If you patted me down you would feel nothing, yet within the garments were US dollars, a cloth map, button compass, scalpel blades, a wire saw, fishing kit, painkillers, water purification pills, a sewing kit, wire snares, lengths of nylon cord, a small knife and so on. If I had the chance to run for it, I could. The next layer was a Colombian army combat vest or chest rig, as they are now commonly referred to. This held more important items like water, first aid kit, navigation aids and a knife. And, lastly, the backpack containing everything else: a change of clothing in the form of a lightweight suit made of parachute material, something dry to sleep in, hammock, machete and food supplies for the jungle phase, more water, camera, and a few other odds and ends. The thinking was that in a thick jungle it's hard to move fast, especially with a backpack. So should the need arise, the backpack would be the first to get ditched, allowing me to run or move faster through dense vegetation with the vest and the most important items. I had sturdy boots and leather gloves to protect my hands. These jungles are just shimmering with needle-sharp thorns and spikes some centimetres long.

As for river mode, the problem I faced was the fact that the rivers in jungles are the highways of the jungle. Everyone uses them as you would a road network, friend and foe alike. I did not know who I would meet on the river. And you are an easy target sitting in the river; there's no quick escape. Luckily for me, nature provided the answer. These jungle rivers had plenty of loose vegetation, mostly mangrove patches floating downstream. So the plan was pretty simple: float north, hiding among mixed floating vegetation. To do this I would use the combat vest with small plastic bottles, so it acted as a life jacket. The backpack would be floated, its contents in plastic bags with floatation provided by large plastic Coke bottles. Then the backpack and I could be camouflaged and hide within the mangroves. Simple.

I walked to the far end of the village, Rio Sucio, used foliage to camouflage my equipment while a soldier and a group of children watched, then simply slipped into the water and began a slow ride north. I watched as Rio Sucio faded out of view, into the background of the forest, thick walls of green on either side of me, albeit at a distance as the river was kilometres wide in parts.

Floating in water all day is an odd way to travel, but it works. The pace is slow, the world is peaceful and at times beautiful. The water below the first foot or so feels quite cool, and when the wind is blowing on the open river it gets choppy and you get cold, which seems strange in a high-humidity jungle at more than 30 degrees Celsius (86 degrees Fahrenheit).

The river was a definite change of pace and I had been surprised by the chilly waters. This was a new experience and a welcome change from the jungle. I surrendered to the flow of the river. I had to travel at the speed it was willing to carry me.

I wasn't alone in the river. There were caimans. Technically, these night-time fish feeders of just a few metres in length are not really interested in humans. However, meeting them nose-to-nose at eye level is always a little uncomfortable. Toward the end of the day, I would make my way to the edge of the river and at night climb out and camp. It could take an hour or so to get to the bank from the centre of the river. Then, before last light, I would find a spot where I could sling the hammock between jungle trees. Unfortunately, right out of the gate, I had picked up an ugly stomach infection from Rio Sucio and was suffering from acute diarrhoea. This was making life very unpleasant. The first evening I was suffering from painful cramps and constant diarrhoea while in the water, where your waste product floats with you. In the hammock at night, I would be faced with a mosquito net literally opaque with frenzied swarms and there was a contest of wills when you have to get out of your hammock to dash for the river in the dark. I really didn't want to; I couldn't face the bloodsuckers in these numbers. So I would procrastinate until the pain was too much. Then, while trying to leave the hammock, I would tense while steadying my balance and that, unfortunately, was not doable in my current condition, resulting in a premature release of waste fluids into the waterproof hammock bed; at which point I would give up and just sleep in my warm pool. You reach a point where you really don't care anymore. In the morning you wash off in the river and float away.

There was a time when I grew so cold in the water that I headed for the banks to get out and warm up in the sun. I crawled onto the muddy bank and lay outstretched to revive. I found I was sharing it with a bunch of crocodiles just down the bank, and realized man and croc had momentarily developed a mutual understanding in a rare, shared experience. Although I'm not cold-blooded like these crocodiles, we both needed our blood warming. Millions of years of evolution were momentarily short-circuited in order for us to share this primitive environment. I smiled to myself, contemplating this bizarre moment, the crocodiles' unflinching cold eyes showing little or no concern.

Like all plans, this one was also less than perfect. Halfway and two days into my river journey, I was passing a small village on the west bank with a scattered collection of huts. I was way out in the middle of the river when one of the empty water bottles I was using for extra buoyancy (that was tucked under the front of the combat vest) worked its way free and popped out. It launched itself, landing just out of arm's length, throwing my bouncy off-kilter and loosening the vest. While fighting to keep the other bottle from escaping, I began rotating in the water. Eventually I brought everything under control.

Looking west at the bank, I could see children running along the shore to the village. I watched as they ran to a group of fishermen. Oh shit, not a lot I could do about that. People manned canoes and began paddling out. I'd no idea what I was facing yet my chances were good. As they approached, the boat hooks were raised and eventually they pulled alongside in a frantic rush to pull me from the water. Imagine their confusion when I resisted, telling my rescuers thanks but no thanks. A rather confusing conversation ensued and eventually I was left to my own devices. I drifted slowly away, staring at two canoes' worth of perplexed faces – did they really find a white guy just drifting down the Atrato River? They watched for a while, and I even gave a wave as I went on my merry way. I sometimes wonder how the villagers' story of the riverman has evolved over time!

––––––––––

On another occasion, at the end of the day, I was trying to clamber up a mud bank for the jungle and doing a very poor job. Caked in mud I would keel, sliding back down, and at one point stopped to get my breath. At that moment a canoe emerged from the reeds with two occupants. They just stared at me with blank faces as they passed and were gone in moments amid the trees. I just kept at it until I made it into the jungle. I cut a clearing and slung the hammock. No sooner had I wrapped up than I could hear shouting. That developed into hearing people cutting into the forest looking for me. I considered breaking camp and making a run for it, but where? Ultimately I decided instead to go out and meet them. Just like my rescuers in the river earlier, their efforts were out of concern for me, apparently. They were delighted to find me and insisted I join them. Unbeknown to me, I had come ashore not far from another small village comprising of *palapas* topped with banana leaves. Yes, your Hollywood-inspired typical vision of a tropical straw hut on a desert island, that's bang on. I was entertained, fed – the standard rice and fish – and we tried exchanging stories of high adventure until late, at which point I crashed in a hut and spent the night being drained of what sickly blood I had left by clouds of insane mosquitoes.

I really felt bad about using their river as my toilet every 15 minutes, but such is life.

The journey continued for four fascinating days – it's one of the most bizarre things I've ever done. Floating close to the banks of the jungle, I would drift beneath tall herons who would just stare at me, clearly unsure of what they were looking at. As I was camouflaged, they could be forgiven. I would pass right below troops of white-face monkeys and howlers, and no creature batted an eyelid at me. I watched ospreys take fish right out of the water in front of me. It was quite a safari ride.

In my camouflage I was able to blend in, to some extent, and become an observer. I guess that's similar to how a wildlife camera operator might feel while sitting in a hide, or how a hunter feels as they try to become one with the backdrop. Although I was still in survival mode, as I had been for the road and first jungle phases, I was able at times to let go and enjoy seeing without being seen. Observing different animals and birds in their natural environment felt like a rare gift.

Finally my GPS and map put me in the right spot and I began the attempt at leaving the river. I could clearly see the high ground now, yet it took several attempts to get free of the river. I found myself trapped behind forests of dense mangroves and waist-deep mud. In short, I failed to leave the river on the first day.

The following day I made better progress and left the river for the next phase, the Darien jungle. The easy part was over.

I realized the enormous effort it was taking to make almost meaningless progress. By the end of the second day, I was a mess, still sick as a dog, and dipping into my rations before I had even reached the jungle. Then I realized I really didn't have enough food, and my daily calorie calculations were clearly not right. This was a low point. It didn't help when I tried to use my camera and found it jammed. The cheap Instamatic plastic camera with rolls of 35mm film had got wet. I tried in vain but ultimately had to make the terrible decision to remove the film that was in the camera, knowing I was about to lose all my footage. It was heartbreaking to think of the amazing photos gone forever – unfortunately, not for the last time.

I was also feeling something I termed 'terrain shock' – the overwhelming, almost claustrophobic, reaction to the jungle. It was tight, in your face and terrible. If you just bent over or turned around, you had no idea where you were going or had just come from. It was incredibly disorientating, on a whole new level. The stomach issues and diarrhoea were also taking a toll. Yet the plan was clear, a direct assault on the jungle using a compass, heading for the border. The next day and the following days I walked 2–3 kilometres (1–2 miles) between dawn and dusk, trying to manoeuvre or beat my way through the Darien. I was already losing the skin off my hands from using the machete. Slow, complicated progress glued to the compass, seemingly perpetually climbing over huge fallen trees one after another. By now I no longer felt the mosquito bites nor the itchiness my body had become accustomed to. I had taken malaria treatment for the first time on my journey in anticipation, as I knew malaria was a concern in the Darien. Life had felt easier in the river and now I missed it. Life in the jungle was unforgiving, exhausting and stressful.

The food soon began to run out and things were not improving. I was fatigued, feeling weak and overwhelmed; the jungle was wearing me down. Sometimes I would find what looked like a track, or something that had been a track once, perhaps. I would find the lure impossible to resist and try to follow it. It's hard to express just how good it felt to be able to move a few metres without great effort. Sometimes you would be unable to decide whether it was a faded track or just a random gap in the jungle, or just your imagination playing tricks on you like a mirage. I would try classing them as weak or strong signals; a strong signal was something that really did look like it could have been a track. Nonetheless, they would always lead you astray; it was a fool's game. Stick to the bearing and endure the jungle. The days crept by slowly, each a mind-numbing endurance event.

My water was a mix of coconut milk, and occasionally I would find a dried-up stream bed where the water was being filtered into crystal-clear small pools by the sands. I had no filter and didn't need one. An added chlorine pill was enough. This was a major benefit of the dry season. In the rainy season these would have been torrents of mud.

And then one day... one sweet day, I stepped out of the shade of the jungle into the sunlight and a river clearing. The mosquitoes refused to follow because they are evil and sunlight kills them. I had happened across crystal-clear pools framed by slabs of smooth sandstone. Beautiful, cool clear bathing pools filled with fish. Literally the garden of Eden. It's hard to express just how much of a morale booster this was. I lay floating in the pools while hundreds of tiny fish nibbled at my body. This was the only part of the world I have known where there was literally no sign of humanity. You saw no evidence of man at all, nothing. No cigarette butt, no can ring-pulls, no plastic bottles, no nothing. It truly was pure and pristine.

I noticed if anything was dropped into the ponds the fish jumped it immediately. This had promise. I unstitched parts of my clothes and removed my survival fishing kit. Using tiny little frogs as bait, before I knew it I was catching edible-sized fish, including catfish, from deeper parts of the stream. I suddenly had the food supply I was in desperate need of. A good-sized fish every 10– 15 minutes became a rack of fish in no time. Being deep down in a valley surrounded by forest, I was willing to light a small fire over which I could cook. Again, it is hard to express how good a meal this was. Come the morning, I took a compass bearing and it was back into the jungle, machete in hand.

These jungles are dominated by ants and termites; the sheer numbers are mind-boggling. At night I would sling my hammock and use Vaseline on the anchor ties on either end to stop the ants from overrunning my bed. I left the backpack beneath it but each morning I would wake to find either ants or termites had moved in and built their version of Los Angeles in the backpack, complete with mud chambers and eggs. The first 10 minutes of every morning was spent beating them from the backpack.

You don't see much wildlife by day – not large animals or even snakes, as they can hear you coming. Monkeys, on the other hand, do come to see you, being curious as they are. However, at night, the jungle is alive and you can hear the most incredible things. Things you can only guess at. It's too dark to see anything, pitch-black, creating quite interesting time alone. I was shocked at how many trees I could hear falling at night; sometimes the sound would be close and startling.

I stumbled across many streams within breaks in the forest, these gardens of Eden complete with a supply of fresh fish. It wasn't long before I was completely dependent on the fish and coconuts. However, I also learned that consuming too much coconut makes you very ill, with its high concentration of saturated fats. By now I was climbing steep hillsides as well as fighting the jungle. I was climbing into the mountains that mark the border with Panama.

It had been ten days since I had left the river. I'd covered a distance that would have taken me only a day on the road. I was watching the GPS closely and now found myself standing on what, by all accounts, should be the border with Panama, slap bang in the middle of the Darien jungle. Then I realized I was leaving South America after more than two years of high-end adventure. Exhausted and cut to ribbons, I remember sitting on the border and sobbing like a child for several minutes. The jungle had given me an ass-whipping.

After my little internal crisis, it was time to start looking for the first waypoint in Panama, the indigenous village of Paya. I found myself on some sort of track running along the border, to the east — maybe at least an animal track. But again, this proved to be futile and led me astray. I suddenly realized I had made a colossal mistake with navigation. I had marked Paya on a map, copied from another map in Medellin, but never actually confirmed a grid reference. In other words, the mark on the map was mostly worthless, a rough guesstimate. I had simply failed to follow through and get the details I needed. A seriously rookie mistake. I remember the sinking feeling and a sense of despair on realizing what I had done. However, it proved to be not a complete loss as it got me close enough. Having spent so long in the jungle, you pick up on subtle differences in your environment. As I homed in on the location, I picked up on signs of human activity and soon stumbled across a felled clearing. That was all I needed. Then I just followed the path of devastation to plantations of banana trees, tracks and, suddenly, through the jungle by a river, I saw a village.

I sat hidden in the jungle and watched for a while. I knew FARC still operated this side of the border, hiding in these mountains. I had no idea who was in this village so I spent some time observing from afar to be sure. Mostly families, children playing, women washing clothes in the river. The village was incredibly neat. The grass was kept like a football pitch, with no trash and tidy huts. I don't know what I was expecting but it was a pleasant surprise, I guess. A sense of order in such sharp contrast to the overwhelming cluster of nature's jungles. Convinced I was safe, I crossed the river and met the Kuna, the indigenous peoples of Panama's Darien.

I ended up staying with the village senior elder and his family. The chief helped Panamanian officials by keeping records of who came that way. In short, not many. In the past they had. Indeed, some time ago there had even been tourism through the Gap, and the more adventurous tourists had taken guided tours into it. I rested for a few days and ate well. I also got a chance to sit and take my camera apart. It had twice failed and I had lost all my footage of the Darien, a disaster that would haunt me for years to come. I found the circuitry coated in a thin film of dirt from the river and scrubbed it clean, whereupon it worked. I took few photos of the family and the village. But the camera kept jamming.

From Paya, there was a simple short track to the next village, Pucoro. I spent the night there and the next morning followed the tracks that splayed out from the Kuna villages in a spider's web-like pattern until I found a river I was looking for. Again, rivers were the key to my travel and, fortunately, all the rivers were flowing in the right direction for me. I was basically amphibious at this point anyhow; in the water, out of the water, it made little difference in the jungle. You would be soaking wet all day, in any case. With my vest and backpack afloat, I simply went on another extended river crossing. By now I was starting to relax, feeling like the worst of it was behind me. I had made it through the Gap, for the most part, made it out of Colombia, avoided FARC, and was feeling far less stressed. For days the river systems wound their way north, and again I lived off the land. I was almost enjoying myself now. Some days the rivers were shallow enough to walk through, and I would pull my floating backpack behind me with rope like a pet dog on a leash. Other days the river would run like a rapid and I would ride the surf, having the time of my life, my cares and worries behind me. I watched birds of paradise above me in the trees as I bobbed my way merrily downstream. Camping by the river at night with a fire and my fish. Stargazing at brilliant night skies.

There are few places in the world, beyond the city lights, where you get a chance to see the night sky and understand it and appreciate it, like our ancestors did. Where we manage to slip the minutia of our day-to-day existence, the small circles of life, and look up and find ourselves being exposed to the enormity of everything else. No distractions, just the flicker of a campfire cooking your fish. These are the things I live for, a quiet moment in awe, mesmerizing and humbling. Spend long enough alone in a jungle and things become very primitive.

Sometimes, not just in the Darien, you'll find you are in a place and time where the only time that matters is the rising and setting of the sun. Harkening back to a time before the tick-tock of a mechanical clock, back to the poetic heavenly motions, the waxing and waning of celestial bodies. We wake when the sun rises, we sleep when the sun sets. There is a reason midnight is called "mid night", a relevance lost to us these days. On the road one forms a primitive relationship with the cycles, the real cycles. Not news cycles, not a cycle around the next Apple product release or elections. But a physical relationship with a basic past.

Crossing the Darien Gap took me two months. The journey into Panama to reach the British Embassy in Panama City proved to be every bit as challenging as escaping Colombia. Encounters at gunpoint with Panama's frontier police would see me spend 18 days in haul before I could emerge from the jungle onto the roads of Central America. Death would have to wait. I had been fortunate to live another life in those two months. Another world and time.

I had been caiman, lived like an amphibian, and become part of an incredible ecosystem, if but for a short time – one of the most memorable moments of my life I will never forget. From time to time I find myself stopping and staring into forests or hedgerows, into a dark, deep-green, nostalgic place, feeling excited with the flicker of adrenaline. There is still time for great adventures.

BREATH

BY LYNX VILDEN

My breath is the wind in its infancy,
Birthed from the place where land meets sky
It searches along the stream banks for leaves left
long before winter.

My breath rimes the swamp grass with hoarfrost
That shatters as it falls, though only the ears of the owl
can hear it
We are crystals, we are crystals transforming

My breath rising from the living burning flame
Ignited in the very beginning
And carried in the chest of every holy torch bearer

My breath a seemingly endless sigh
That cloaks barren mountains and whispers
I have come … I have come home.

Lynx has travelled, explored and researched traditional cultures around the world.

Currently based in Norway, she is the founder of Living Wild, teaching Stone Age living skills to help people connect with nature and build resilience.

David is the creator and co-founder of Color the Water, a California based anti-racist surf community for all Black, Indigenous, and People of Color (BIPOC). He is first generation Filipino American, grew up far from the beaches of Southern California and yet found a way to teach himself at age 21, and has always wanted a surf culture that better reflects surfing's melanated origins. After over a decade of international work, travel, and surfing around the world and experiencing more equitable surf cultures both in people and practice, David returned to California in 2020 amidst the pandemic and at the height of racial tensions in America with a deep determination to spark change.

This describes a key encounter that cemented some of the ideas that would become the foundation of Color the Water, particularly how joyful practices in nature can help heal racial trauma as well as the deep ancestral wounds people of color of carry in their relationship with the ocean.

COLOR THE WATER: WINSTON

DAVID MALANA

I'd never surfed Venice Breakwater before, but for some reason that day it seemed like the place to go. Walking to the break, feeling the mixture of terrains soften under my bare feet – asphalt, concrete, grass, sand – my clenched jaw and furrowed brow also softened. It was one of those bright yet not bright, cold, overcast summer days, as it had been for a while. All these years away from California and I'd forgotten that "June Gloom" was a thing. The air felt charged and heavy. The sand and shore had medical masks strewn all over them. Such was the surf scene of 2020. I placed my board down and stretched while I looked out to the ocean. There were a lot of people, mostly white men, as usual. The waves were on the bigger side, and a sea of sizzling foam drifted north. It was a mixture of white, yellow and green, like the bubbling foam of boiled chicken. The ocean always looks so much scarier when the sun is not out, I thought to myself. I slapped my leash against my leg to shake off sand, wrapped it snug around my ankle, and walked into the ocean with my board tucked under my arm, wax side facing me.

I need this right now. I'll get back to the struggle of fighting systemic racism, but right now, I just need to surf, I thought. The ocean did not cooperate. The current was strong and the waves were too frequent to paddle out unscathed. Wave after wave smashed into me, enveloping my entire body, starting to impact directly into my face. I imagined this is how a baby must feel when their parents are vigorously washing their face and they can barely breathe. There's a certain burn in the shoulders that comes with constant paddling that is exacerbated when you realize the ocean has you moving in the opposite direction to what you intend. As I plunged my arms into the water again and again, pulling myself toward the horizon, other senses started to activate. I became aware of this multilayered soundscape of the sloshing and slapping of my arms and the board, the fizzling of foam that only comes when waves are crashing extra hard, and the undertones of reverberation and echo that come from the ocean from all directions and distances. That part sometimes reminds me of auditoriums and churches. The smell of the ocean in Los Angeles is a mixture of salt, sea creatures and subtle smells of trash. The diffused light of the midday sun hitting the cloud cover reminded me of the photography lessons I used to do. Nature's soft box, I recalled. I paddled for what felt like half an hour. It took all of my 20 years of ocean experience and what little physical fitness I had to make it. Panting, I straddled my board, sat up and looked around.

I was still paddling on the treadmill of a current that was taking me away from the waves, stubbornly fighting against it. There's a certain rhythm that comes with entering the ocean once the shock wears off and the body realizes that the elements and the nature of its current existence are aquatic. Some days, finding that rhythm is harder than others. This was one of those days. However, a few surfers seemed perfectly at ease, catching waves near the rocks and riding expertly past them, and paddling back out in what seemed like a different, calmer ocean than the rest of us. How do they make it look so easy? I thought to myself. They must surf here all the time. They are probably locals. Must be nice. I looked back to the beach to see how far I'd drifted. The parallax of trees to buildings was moving fast as I sat still, and the wind was moving through the trees in a direction that indicated that the surf would soon get more turbulent. While looking back I also saw something I'd never seen before, but a wave came before I could dedicate much attention to it.

I'd been paddling against the current for what felt like forever, and finally I was in a position to catch a wave. An undulating rise of the horizon indicated that a wave was on the way. I scanned to each side of it – first for formations that would indicate which direction to ride, then for people to see if anyone was already in position closer than where I was. As the wave came, I could feel the energy of the ocean start to rise underneath me. From my seated position, I twirled my legs like vertical propellers under the water to rotate my board. I then lay prone on the board, facing the beach, hoping to have enough paddle energy to match the speed of the energy moving through the water. I looked back to see the wave approaching. It lifted me from behind; that critical moment arrived. I paddled deeply and strongly, and my legs started to kick. The sound of the tops of my feet splashing against the cresting face of the wave indicated that it was time to stand up. I stopped paddling, placed my hands under my rib cage, and tried to propel my upper body just enough to tuck my legs and place my feet flat on the board.

A moment of suspenseful quiet felt both instant and prolonged as the wave crest pitched over in the moments right before it crashed. The only feeling I've ever been able to compare it to is that moment right at the top of a rollercoaster when the clanking ends and it's just silent. I tucked my legs, placed my feet, released my hands, and looked down at the face of the wave. It was much steeper than I was prepared for. The board, which had been lifted nearly vertical, was headed straight into the water at high speed. I wasn't going to make it. I pushed off and away from the board and plunged downward into the water, body balled up and face covered. The ripping sound of the plunge gave way to a deep, muffled gurgle, as if the ocean were swishing me around in her mouth. I tumbled underneath the surface, surrendering to the swirling darkness as the wave pulled me deeper down. It will let go soon, I assured myself. Sure enough, the gurgling subsided and the light reaching my closed eyelids turned lighter. I reached my hands upward and outward and pulled them down. I did the same with my legs. I broke the surface of the water with just my head and took a deep breath. All I could see was white, like a camera exiting a dark tunnel. As my eyes adjusted, I looked toward the beach and saw a large group of people. They were sitting in a single line as far as the eye could see. Dressed in all black, I could see what looked like signs, drums and cameras. It was a protest.

They were there because of George Floyd, whose murder by police in Minneapolis just a short time before had been videoed in broad daylight for a world in pandemic lockdown to see. I had gone to a couple of peaceful protests in the form of paddle outs, where dozens of mostly white surfers gathered with surfboards adorned with "Black Lives Matter" and "Say His Name" in paint and tape. I vowed at those paddle outs to make fighting racism part of my daily life. This looked different from those. Wait, should I join this thing? Should I be protesting, too? I'd been surfing for at least an hour and my parking meter was going to run out soon. I'd caught a couple of waves — most had caught me — and I felt like it was time to go. I let the drift pull me in, closer to shore where the waves subsided before they broke again. It was calm there, quieter, off to the side of the ocean's aquatic concert. I saw a man there, struggling to try and catch waves that were not going to break. The calmness of the water made me aware of how cold I was, and also how hungry. That was my indication that it was time to go. This man, though, was someone I couldn't turn away from. It was so rare to see a Black person in the ocean with the intention of teaching themselves how to surf. I paddled over to him and sat down on my board.

"Hey man, the current is intense today, eh? I think the tide is rising, too, and the onshore winds are making it kind of choppy." I glided my hands back-and-forth along the surface of the water as I did my best impression of surf small talk.

"Man, I don't know about any of that," he said frankly. "I'm just out here trying to figure this out."

"Ah, okay. Good luck," I said sheepishly.

Should I have offered some advice? I didn't want to come across as patronizing but I knew there were some things I could help with. I didn't want him to think that I was just singling him out because he's Black, either. But the truth is, I was. Is that a bad thing? My mind was racing. The idea of offering surf lessons and media to people of colour had come to me during the paddle outs, but I didn't have any way of finding anyone to teach besides my nieces.

By then, I'd paddled in and it was shallow enough to stand. As I made my way to shore, I could see that the line of people protesting extended from Santa Monica Pier all the way to Venice Pier, about 5 kilometres (3 miles). I walked through them, situating my board in a way that they could see the "BLM" I had smeared on with wax. Something about that felt strange and wrong. The wet sand under my feet crunched as my heels sank, and then my toes, with each step. A photographer asked me if he could take a photo. I paused and stood still. This is what you wanted, right, David? This is why you put that BLM on the board. Why does it feel shameful, then? Why do I feel like an imposter? The reverse process of walking from sand to grass, from concrete to asphalt returned my clenched jaw and furrowed brow. You should have said something to that surfer. You should have asked him if he wanted help. The water dripping down my wetsuit onto my feet wasn't enough to rinse my feet, but it felt cool and soothing as I peeled the suit down. It's not too late. You can still go up to him and at least offer. With a towel wrapped around my waist, I could now feel the cool onshore winds against my skin and the smell of churros and weed from the boardwalk stores. I told myself if he says no, he says no, but at least you won't have to live with regret for the rest of your life wondering "What if?" At least you'll know it's not because you didn't try. The strength of the sun, though still covered by clouds, made me squint as I looked back to the beach. Just ask him if he wants photos or videos of himself. He'll probably say no, and you can come right back. Your meter won't run out by then. I put on my clothes, grabbed my camera, and scurried back out toward the beach.

As I walked once more from urban land to coastal sand, I could see the line of people starting to coalesce. I was rushing, and sand from the back of my sandals was coming dangerously close to my camera. It looked like the protestors in Venice were gradually starting to make their way over to Santa Monica, almost one by one standing and becoming part of a slow, growing crowd. I looked for the man I'd seen earlier and couldn't find him in the water. My quickened pace slowed and I dropped my head. I felt like I had missed my chance. I looked one last time out to the beach and I saw him on the shore, sitting. Slowly I approached him from behind, sitting what I estimated to be 2 metres (6 feet) away.

"Hey man, how was it out there?" I asked tentatively.

"Man, I don't even know, I am just trying to figure this thing out," he replied.

"Yeah, it's tricky today. So … how are you doing, with all this … you know." I gestured toward the protest.

It was a risk to ask such a thing, but I didn't know what else to do. I sat in the sand with my arms hugging my crossed legs and listened to him as he told me how much all this hurt. The crashing waves sent wafts of ocean mist toward us as I told him how deeply hurt I felt that Black people were being treated so inhumanely. I nodded my head as I noticed the streams of water forming from the sides of his face down his legs, onto the shore and back into the ocean, as he graciously explained to me why Black on Black crime statistics are skewed and how even if it exists on any level, it is still a symptom of white supremacy and systemic racism. We spoke for over an hour, sitting there, as the tide continued to rise and started to touch his feet.

"Thank you so much for talking with me. It means more to me than I can say. I don't know if you would be interested, but I have my camera and could take some video of you surfing that might be useful for learning later, if you want," I offered.

"Yeah, sure," he replied.

"By the way, I'm David."

"Nice to meet you, David. I'm Winston." He put his leash back on and walked into the ocean.

The second time around, the water is always colder. I was only knee deep, but I could feel the difference. Winston was out trying to catch waves but was having trouble. Waves breaking on shore would rush up to me and jump toward my clothes and camera, as if they were using my feet as ramps. I looked to the left of me to see the group of people continuing to grow and approach. The sound of the water rushing up the shore was high, like a magazine swiftly gliding across a coffee table. Winston was too far back on his board to catch waves. I was trying to physically signal to him to scoot forward, to no avail. The bottom of my shorts was wet as I propped my camera over my head. After a few waves, I waved my arm toward the shore, asking if he could come in.

"Can I show you a couple videos and offer some tips?" I asked.

"Of course," he said. We both looked at the screen of the camera, which was difficult because of all the reflections of the sky.

"So if you scoot up a little, so that the board rests a little flatter on the water, when the white water hits you, you may have enough speed to stand and continue on the rest of the wave. Try to make sure you're not standing on the back of the board. That's like the brakes."

We were standing close to each other, both about thigh deep in the water. I could feel the coarse sand under and around my feet, and the water from his chin and ear dripping onto my arm. A commotion behind us had us both look back. The crowd was getting closer and starting to chant things we couldn't yet make out. Winston went back into the water.

"NO JUSTICE! NO PEACE!" The chants of the crowd grew.

The wind seemed to calm a bit, which let the chants carry all the way out into the ocean. Winston positioned himself a little further along than where he was before. He looked back and I gave him a thumbs up.

"SAY HIS NAME!" Surfers looked back, and most continued surfing.

A wave approached and Winston spun his board around. I positioned my camera, planted my feet, and crouched into a half-squat to try to get a lower angle. The sand gave way to my forefeet, cool and coarse under the callouses I'd formed.

"GEORGE FLOYD!"

The wave Winston chose crashed hard in front of him at a safe enough distance so that by the time it reached him, it was a strong but manageable wave of white water. I could feel where he was in the ocean. I remembered back to some of my first white-water waves and that rush of cold water that thrashes you from behind. The wave hit him, but he kept paddling while maintaining his balance. I leaned my chin forward a bit in the hope he would do the same. The wave thrust him forward and he worked his way up - two hands, up to two feet, repositioned front foot further forward. He was riding the wave!

"ABOLISH THE POLICE!" The crowd was directly behind us.

The roar of their chants seemed to converge with the roar of the waves, interwoven with my own screams of jubilation at the sight of Winston's wave. He peeked at me and smiled a little. The board wobbled at that moment, and he refocused his attention. The interaction of his weight, the board and the water were something I felt so deeply attuned to. His wave finished, he jumped off the board and submerged into the deep water. I screamed again with knees bent and both arms raised. He emerged from the water with a triumphant arm in the air.

"NO JUSTICE, NO PEACE!" could be heard faintly now. The crowd had passed us and was heading toward Santa Monica Pier.

Winston caught a few more wonderful waves, all with the same adjustments we spoke of, all ending with a deeply joyful and renewed energy to ride more. The water on the bottom of my shorts had started to dry, and I felt chilled by the winds that had suddenly picked up. Winston rode one last wave in, on his stomach, looking directly at me and smiling. I stayed focused on him through my camera, one eye squinted and one open into the viewfinder. I zoomed in on his face. Behind his grin I noticed his eyes were red. I became aware of the moisture that had welled up under my own. I lowered my camera and we looked at each other. I wanted to hug him. I wanted to feel the water from his wetsuit soak into my clothes and let him know that I didn't care if I got wet. Instead, I offered the unusual gesture of a fist bump, which was still so connected to Barack Obama as it transitioned to a safe salutation in the time of Coronavirus.

"David ... thank you."

"Man, what?! No ... thank you!"

We exchanged numbers and I asked him if he would be okay if I shared the videos and a potential voiceover on my social media for the idea I had called Color the Water.

"Maybe seeing you might inspire other people of colour to try," I said. "Maybe this can be a way we can share some of the things we talked about while also creating some much-needed representation."

"Absolutely, man. Just let me know," Winston said.

I smiled as I walked back to my car. The hard asphalt replaced the soft sand, but my jaw remained unclenched and my brow unfurrowed. I put my camera in the passenger seat, closed my door, and just as I started to turn the ignition I looked up and saw a parking ticket on my car. This is the best 63 motherfucking dollars I have ever spent, I thought to myself! I drove the hour-long journey home excited, joyful and proud.

Little did I know, the video that would come from that chance encounter would help turn Color the Water from a hopeful hashtag, to a small informal group, to an official non-profit organization, seeking racial justice and liberation as a community of hundreds of anti-racist surfers of colour. That protest wound up being the start of the Santa Monica riots. The Venice beach area would become my home of two years and running, and the central location from where Color the Water continues to offer free lessons, media and also community to all Black, indigenous and people of colour. Little did I know that the surfers who I met and who I joined at the beginning of it all would end up helping build Color the Water into more than a service, more than a community, more than a safer space — a movement. Little did I know that my most beloved, joyful connection with nature — the ocean — would beget the space in which I would have the chance to fight for what I believe in, with people I admire.

There is a healing power in the ocean that our ancestors of colour revered and hallowed. Wave sliding was created by ancient civilizations of colour in ancient Polynesia, Peru and Africa as a form of spiritual and communal practice. Over time, as colonization and the symptoms of systemic racism pervaded throughout the world, surfing lost both its reverent roots and its connection to communities of colour. It's become something aggressive, commodified, territorial and exclusionary. Now more than ever, as the people of the world reconcile their relationship to nature, it is important that we reject this colonized surf culture and reconnect people of colour to the ocean in ways that dismantle the systems of oppression that have marginalized us away from it, and also heal from the generational trauma that systemic racism has had us undergo. That is the mission of Color the Water, to be a space of celebration, reverence, intention and healing. Our most powerful tool against the evils of systemic racism and all oppression is the defiant love and joy that we can nurture in our whole selves — embracing the differences of our identities while removing the hierarchy that white supremacy has placed on those differences. With the ocean as our sanctuary and the waves as our safe space, we believe we can find liberation for ourselves and, hopefully one day, for us all.

I DON'T KNOW WHAT WILL KILL US FIRST: THE RACE WAR OR WHAT WE'VE DONE TO THE EARTH

FATIMAH ASGHAR

so I count my hopes: the bumblebees
are making a comeback, one snug tight
in a purple flower I passed to get to you;
your favorite color is purple but Prince's
was orange & we both find this hard to believe;
today the park is green, we take grass for granted
the leaves chuckle around us; behind
your head a butterfly rests on a tree; it's been
there our whole conversation; by my old apartment
was a butterfly sanctuary where I would read
& two little girls would sit next to me; you caught
a butterfly once but didn't know what to feed it
so you trapped it in a jar & gave it to a girl
you liked. I asked if it died. you say you like
to think it lived a long life. yes, it lived a long life.

Originally published online in Poem-a-Day on 8 May 2019, by the Academy of American Poets (poet.org).

Fatimah is a poet, fiction writer and film maker from the USA who explores and pushes the boundaries of identity, relationships and humanity – exploring themes of race, sexuality and religion.

Leaving her home in Oregon and walking more than 32,000 kilometres (20,000 miles) across 14 countries on 4 continents, Angela discovered her innate strength and courage. She faced the odds of surviving the outback in Australia, dengue fever in Vietnam and the sheer challenges of being a woman sleeping alone in a tent. It was an experiment of living on less and following her heart, lasting nearly seven years. She has been featured in Lonely Planet, Outside and BBC Travel, among other publications.

This is her story about crossing the Australian desert, who she met and what affected her deeply.

DESERT SOLACE

ANGELA MAXWELL

Red sand filled every crevice of my tent and body. My skin was painted terracotta and the easterly winds had shaped my naturally untamed hair into a few thick strands of knotted rope. I was struggling to keep a symbiotic relationship with the sun without new sunburn blisters forming. The trees were thin and spindly with no shade to be offered. The landscape was filled with human-sized termite mounds and only in the late afternoon could I find a shady refuge next to one of them as the sun began its bedtime routine.

Just five months earlier I had been living in a cosy little cottage in Oregon, reading about other people's adventures and daydreaming about one I might have. I drove to the grocery store, met friends for coffee downtown and ordered pizza deliveries on Saturday nights. I had two credit cards I still hadn't paid off and had a decent career managing my own business. Life was pretty good. I had no reason to jostle it up. That is, until I had the idea to walk my way around the world, alone. Every step of the way.

Yes, you're absolutely correct if you think that's as mad an idea as you've ever heard before. It's quite honestly crazy. It's an enormous undertaking and possibly a highly treacherous endeavour, albeit a daydreamer's fantasy. And I had zero experience in how to survive anything beyond my own backyard.

But I couldn't shake off the idea.

I would walk the streets and imagine passing the Taj Mahal, and as I curved around the next corner there was a tropical jungle, then a Grecian island. It went on for a few months like this, me harbouring this secret desire to go on a walkabout clear round the globe. I didn't say anything to anyone but I began devouring biographies of different explorers and female adventurers. I read about Gertrude Bell and her archaeological expeditions. I followed Jane Goodall through the African forest and ran with Rosie Swale-Pope as she trudged through the Siberian winter. I travelled the wilderness of the world through their words of trial and error, defeat and triumph. And even though all of them had had very different types of adventures, there was one common thread that sparked my daydream into hope. The commonality in all their stories was that it all began with an idea and a willingness to take a risk and follow their heart. And adventure doesn't ask us for a resumé or how many years' experience we have had. It asks us if we're willing to step into the unknown.

So although I was fully aware that walking alone around the world seemed crazy, especially since I had zero expertise in anything related to outdoor survival, camping and long-distance walking, my lack of knowledge and experience wasn't a good enough reason for me to ignore the idea altogether.

I mean, I didn't have to learn how to walk. I wasn't aiming for speed or to break any records. I didn't need to take an exam or pass a test. What I didn't know, I could learn. And where I didn't have even the smallest inkling of experience, I could gain some.

And that was that. It was through a 7-kilogram (15-pound) stack of autobiographies, some motivational YouTube speeches on how you can do anything you put your mind to and some late-night map planning that I committed to walk my way around the world.

Five months ago when I had left the suburbs of Perth to make my way along the Indian Ocean coast, I was still a complete novice. I knew the salty air and towering paperbark trees would soon be replaced with hot wind gusts and low shrubs. I also knew that as soon as I had left the greenery for the terracotta desert, finding water and shade would be the most vital part of surviving. I had a water filter but that didn't come with a water diviner. I honestly didn't know how I was going to find water in one of the harshest deserts in the world.

As my finger skimmed the paper map tracing the coastal route that would take me through Cervantes, Geraldton and Kalbarri National Park, I knew I had about a month before my trail would deposit me on dusty roads. It seemed like a good amount of time to get some outdoor skills under my belt. I would have to be smart about my decisions and learn to conserve my water. I ambled closer to the outback while anxiously eyeing my two 10-litre (2-gallon) dromedary bags with every sip of water I consumed. Thankfully, I was still near scattered seaside villages and finding a waterspout was fairly easy. But I wasn't naive to the fact that water dispensaries didn't exist in the lonely desert.

My nervousness was soothed by listening to a playlist of songs on my phone and as the population of people grew smaller, my voice grew louder. I began singing aloud and even dancing to give my monotonous stride a break.

It was in the chorus of a Cranberries song that I belted a high note and as I looked over to my left, I saw a man standing between some bushes. I was startled and embarrassed all at the same moment. Firstly, I have a horrific singing voice, but I also felt scared about seeing a stranger in the wilderness, standing there looking at me like he knew I was coming. I was completely alone; it was just him and me.

My slack jaw and pounding heart persisted as a smile grew on his dark face and he padded over to me, his bare feet moving across the dry ground. There was the occasional passing car but my confidence that one would pass in the very moment I may need help seemed slim.

"Are you the walking lady?" he asked as he held out his hand for a friendly shake.

"Oh, um, well, I am a lady and I'm walking," I hesitantly replied.

"Yeah, I've heard about you. I've passed through some towns where I've been asked if I've met the woman walking up north."

"Ah. That might be me then." I managed an awkward smile.

"I also go by foot. But right now, I am on a bike", he stated.

I wanted to end the conversation and just carry on, when he invited me to join him to camp a few miles up the road.

"I'm not going much further up the road if you'd like to share a campfire and a meal."

Now, of course, I had red flags waving in my head. Join a complete stranger to camp near each other in the bush? In my head I declined, but I was still dealing with a lifelong addiction to people-pleasing and said I'd keep an eye out for him. I felt I had been cordial but knew that if I saw any sign of him, I would just pass on by and hope to go unnoticed.

Two hours later as the sun was threatening to set, I caught the faintest whiff of grilling meat. It stopped me in my tracks. My diet consisted of 2-minute noodles and bland oatmeal. My mouth watered, and as I got closer I saw the roaring fire and the stranger's figure sitting next to it. I stood still for a long time, just watching the fire from a distance and smelling the flesh roasting. My mind argued incessantly. Was it safe to join him? Would I get any sleep in my tent knowing a stranger was only a few feet away? Would anyone hear me if I needed help?

My hungry stomach and lure of the warm fire won me over. I also reminded myself that part of this adventure was to meet new people. Stay vigilant but walk with an open heart.

I pulled my 45-kilogram (100-pound) two-wheeled cart over a sandy floor and tree debris. He barely flinched as I approached. He stayed seated next to the fire, rolling a handmade cigarette. He nodded in recognition of my arrival and poked the foil-wrapped chops.

We sat around the fire nibbling our dinner, speaking softly and seldomly. He was a man of few words but carried a deep love and knowledge of his surroundings. I could tell by his distinct facial features that he was a native Australian. His hair had a blonde hue to it, which I later learned came from German ancestry.

He made a trip up north every summer by foot or by bike, living off the land and as little as possible. We were headed in the same direction.

That night by the fireside was the beginning of my two weeks with a bushman.

He drank white wine diluted with water and never wore shoes. I decided to call him B for barefoot, which he took to kindly and felt the endearing nature in which I intended it.

B spent two weeks with me and taught me more or less everything I would need to know to survive the outback.

He moved at my slow pace of 24 kilometres (15 miles) a day. He would ride his bike ahead to find a hidden camp spot for us. He left a small orange flag covered with stones on the ground to let me know where to head into the bush to find him. He often had a fire going and a meal cooking by the time I discovered our secret nightly hideout.

B taught me things like how to cover my tracks using leaves and twigs. He once showed me how to harvest feathers from a deceased galah bird we found and then offered its carcass to a meat-ant colony. There were many things B shared with me in our time together, but it seemed he had one more thing to teach me.

Early one evening, before we parted ways, he asked me to follow him. We tramped through dense trees and tall thorny bushes. I thought he was leading me to some watering hole or to help him carry an animal he'd found. Maybe this was where he'd show me how he skinned a dead kangaroo to make a blanket. I was excited for what he was going to show me.

He stopped abruptly in his tracks and I nearly collided with him.

He turned to me and said, "Now, guide us back to camp."

With confusion and wide eyes, I replied, "But I was following you. I wasn't paying attention to our route."

B had no expression on his face as he said, "Always. Pay. Attention."

I had been busy watching his leather-like soles tramp confidently over the prickly ground. I was mesmerized by his stealth and quickness, and I had tripped several times trying to keep up. I wondered what his upbringing may have been like. Did he always walk barefoot? Did he roam free in the wild desert as a boy? Did he go through a walkabout ritual?

He stood with his arms folded as he waited for me to lead us. I turned around to where I thought we had come from and after just five steps he cleared his throat. I looked back at him and he was pointing with his eyes in the opposite direction that I had been heading. Gratefully I began walking in the direction he'd hinted. Though not very much further on I knew I was lost and felt frustrated. I sat on a log and took a few deep breaths. His bare feet were next to me and suddenly I felt envy. I wanted to feel that connection to the ground, to the sandy soil and the roots; a connection that gave him unwavering confidence in how and where he walked.

I knew I didn't yet understand that level of connection to the earth but it must have begun somewhere. At some point. I took off my shoes and closed my eyes.

In my mind, I asked to be guided. I felt the breeze between my sweaty toes and sunk my heels into the sand. I opened my heart and asked the earth to speak to me, to give me some sense of direction.

At first I felt a little silly, but then I remembered how as a child I would stand where the ocean waves lapped over my feet and crashed against my shins. I would look out over the endless blue in the hope of seeing a dolphin. I would send out a silent prayer to the sea while keeping my eyes eagerly set on anywhere a dolphin might make its graceful jump from water into the open air. And sometimes, they appeared. My heart would pound, and I'd squeal with joy. Were the dolphins fulfilling my desire and putting on a show just for me? Most likely it was because it was the migration season. But I was there, waiting and watching. And I felt a connection to the ocean, to the dolphins and, ultimately, to myself.

I opened my eyes and began taking slow and deliberate steps. I would wince when I felt a prickly thorn or protruding rock, but I would keep moving. Occasionally I would stop and listen; not with my ears but with my feet.

The sun had almost completely set and I had no idea how long we had been walking. I felt B's patience and that encouraged me to take my time, even though the impending darkness made me feel worried, even scared. If I had been alone and didn't know how to find my tent again, I would truly be lost, out of water and with no shelter. I felt the real danger of what could happen at times when I wasn't paying attention.

B leaned close to my ear and whispered, "Keep listening." I closed my eyes again and took a deep breath. For a moment, it felt like I was pulled underground. I could hear the termites gnawing and mice digging. I could sense how quiet it all seemed from above, but underneath there was so much life and movement. I wasn't sure if I'd just imagined it all but it was the first time I truly felt connected to Mother Nature. I wanted to trust that I was being guided and held by this world underneath the skin of my feet.

I opened my eyes and felt an urge to go right. We walked and walked until we reached a corrugated dirt road. I remembered this road. It was the road I was following north. Reaching this road meant we had gone too far. I hadn't successfully found our camp. I felt discouraged. Maybe I just didn't have a good sense of direction. Maybe this was a sign that I was already failing at finding my own way. And maybe I didn't really have what it takes to make it all the way around the globe.

When I turned to look at B, he had a smile on his face. I barely knew him but he didn't seem like the kind of person to say I told you so. He simply nodded, turned and pointed. I squinted my eyes as I searched between thick trees and an identical-looking landscape. I was confused.

"Red." That's all he said. One word. Red?

I squinted even more and thought maybe by crouching down and moving my head at different angles like a dog listening intently, I'd see what he saw.

I heard him give a gentle sigh and he began walking in that direction. I followed. I kept my eyes peeled for red. Within a few minutes I finally saw it. A small, no, three small red reflective strips. They were steady, motionless. But they got stronger as we got closer. The silhouette of our tents took shape. We weren't that far from our camp.

Although I didn't get us to the exact location of our camping spot that evening, his lesson in being diligent about my surroundings would stay with me across four continents.

And so there I was, just three weeks later, in the western corner of the Australian outback, in a tango performance with the unforgiving heat. My mouth was perpetually dry and water no longer satisfied my thirst. I hadn't seen another human in three weeks and the last person I did see felt inclined to remind me how many people die each year of heatstroke in the desert.

My arms were covered in blisters, and I was so sure the only reason I hadn't run into any wild dingoes was because my smell had become so offensive.

Yet, as I tucked myself next to a termite mound and watched the sun go down on the desolate desert horizon, I realized I was the happiest I'd ever been in my life.

Each morning was filled with a cacophony of kookaburras and kingfishers, a golden hue waking me from a deep, silent slumber and beckoning me to join the early-bird special with a cup of coffee and a view of the rising sun. The coolness of the night would soon be gone as the first rays of sun began warming all that dwelled in the flat steppes of the outback.

The further north I went, the earlier I had to start walking to avoid the heat. After a coffee and some oatmeal, I would begin packing up my tent and belongings, pressing them down into the one big duffle bag that sat on my two-wheeled cart. Once all my gear was safely tucked inside, I strapped on my bags of water and began making my way through the desert. I would avoid areas of thick sand as my cart became almost impossible to manoeuvre. Pulling the weight of my survival gear through sand felt like pushing a car out of a ditch. I often navigated corrugated dirt roads used by locals between towns. I tried avoiding people, if possible. Although I felt there would be no humans wanting to live in this boiling landscape, there were aboriginal communities and mining camps, as well as truck drivers delivering essentials to replenish the remote villages.

Most of the time I felt very alone. Not in a sad kind of way but in a pleasant way. By being with myself and having no other choice, I began to hear my thoughts more clearly and feel my emotions without judgement. My inner voice became stronger. I began to understand that this is what many people mean by "knowing yourself".

Spending time in nature and listening to my heart – as I did with the crickets and the birds – saw the self-doubt and criticism I had carried through my teens and twenties quieting, and a new voice shone through. My own inner voice. A voice that told me I was capable of anything I wanted to do. A voice that said I was strong, beautiful and independent. A voice that reminded me that although I had no experience in walking alone across vast distances, I was doing it. And I was enjoying it unlike anything else I had done before.

I made a vow to listen to that voice above all else. When I hit a fork in the road, I listened to whether I should go left or right. I began trusting more in myself and my abilities.

After all, I needed to as I still had a very long way to go – another three continents and six years to walk and have to continue to trust in myself. It would never be easy; in fact, it would be the most challenging thing I'd ever do. I had sandstorms and snow blizzards awaiting me, dengue fever in Vietnam and windstorms in Wyoming. But I also had lifelong friends to meet, and strangers who would take me in and offer me food and shelter. There were farmers in need of a helping hand and families ready to share their stories.

On the last day of my walk in Australia I had made it to the coastal town of Honeymoon Bay in Kalumburu. I stood and stared at the turquoise waters as my eyes watered with joy and even a little disbelief. I had just walked over 3,000 kilometres (2,000 miles) to get here. Mostly everyone had doubted me but here I stood at the finishing line.

To get here, I let go of who I thought I was and let myself become the person I wanted to be. I found my voice, my inner strength and self-confidence.

If I could survive walking across Australia, I knew I could walk anywhere. The world was ready for me and I was ready for the world.

THE HUNTER-GATHERER WAY

A family of baboons came down to drink on the opposite side of the river and when they had finished, they disappeared into the bush and a family of smaller animals appeared and they drank and disappeared too, and then a family of even smaller ones came and so on. They came in their kind, bowed their heads and drank, then retreated silently into the bush.

In the middle of the river, large birds swooped down and skimmed the surface of the water with their beaks, then smaller birds flew down, then in the very last of light, the tiniest birds flew down to drink and then they too flew away into the deepening darkness.

Witnessing the reverent procession, this holy communion, I realised that it had happened every evening and before every dawn since the beginning and that not so long ago, there had been a place for people in it, too. We had once known what it felt like to be no greater and no lesser than anyone else. It gave me such a huge sense of relief when I realized that we don't have to rule the world at all, it all works very well, all by itself.

From *The Hunter-Gatherer Way* by Ffyona Campbell, Wild Publishing, 2012. Permission granted by Wild Publishing.

Ffyona is a wild-food teacher from Devon, UK, who was taught by Aborigines, Bushmen and Pygmies on her 20,000-mile walk around the world, which she began at the age of 16.

Born in Sudan, Hamza moved to the UK when he was young and now lives in a rural part of the west coast of Scotland. He is a wildlife cameraman, best known for his TV work on *Countryfile* and *Animal Park*, and has also been a presenter on *Scotland: My Life in the Wild* and children's TV show *Let's Go for a Walk*. In 2022, he was a contestant on the BBC primetime TV show *Strictly Come Dancing*.

He dedicates his life to sharing the wonders of the natural world, in a hope that people will be moved to do their bit for conservation.

In this piece he talks about the trials and tribulations of filming on a remote peninsula and the insights that gave him into life in the wild.

MY EAGLE BROTHER

HAMZA YASSIN

With a mackerel in her talons, the mother sits and waits — beckoning, coaxing the chick that's sitting in the nest the size of a double-bed mattress. It's as if she's saying, "Yeah, why don't you just stretch your wings and hop to me? It's easy." She's been trying to coax him for a number of days. Her motherly patience amazes me. Every so often she adjusts her position to catch the chick's attention, and he stops calling to her for just a moment. But as soon as he realizes she's not coming, he starts calling again, his little neck outstretched toward her, his beak wide.

There's a gust of wind and the trees sway elegantly. The sound of the leaves trembling is soothing, and I feel a breeze through the side of the tent, cooling my skin.

The fish's iridescent skin catches the sunlight. She would have had to fight for this mackerel. She harassed the gannets after their dive, flying at them, scaring them, until one coughed it up and dropped it. She would have caught it in her talons and flown with it all the way back to the nest. Mackerel are delicious and provide much nourishment for her young — but they swim too deep for her to catch. So following the instincts and skills developed by a lineage of her species, she watched the gannets then stole the fish she knew her chick needed. A tantalizing treat that may lure him from the nest.

My fingers tremble on the camera and my eyes twitch. I am waiting for a sign from the chick that he's about to fledge. A flap of a wing, a move to the edge of the nest. But he just sits there, calling for her to bring him food. He's not yet brave enough to make the move.

As I sit there, watching mother and son, I get flashbacks of my own childhood – flashbacks of my mother teaching me to swim. As I would take a stroke toward her arms she would step back, and I would have to take another stroke, coughing and spluttering. She was smiling at me, her skin sparkling and wet. Yes, it would feel as if she was tricking me, but look, soon I was swimming on my own! That was how I learned. It's a technique that all sorts of species use, that gentle coaxing. If you do your homework, you can have a gold star. Isn't that a similar thing?

I've been waiting eight weeks for this event, and I'm aware I could miss it in an instant. My mouth is dry. I haven't dared take a sip of water for a number of hours. My fish fingers, cold and untouched, remain in my lunchbox. It's probably around mid-afternoon. There are still many more hours before Jonny will come up the hill to meet me and help me carry all of this kit back home. My hair lies heavy down my back and there are beads of sweat on my forehead. I feel adrenaline racing around my body – exactly what I need to ensure I stay awake and alert for however long it takes.

My life has become completely intertwined with this family of white-tailed eagles over two months. I've spent around 18 hours a day here, sitting in my tent halfway up a hill, watching their nest. It's a huge nest, high up in a humungous larch, made of tree branches rather than twigs. I'm here to document something that no wildlife camera operator has ever done before: the story of a chick's development from hatching to fledging.

So far I've captured many beautiful events. Although I couldn't see the hatching of the chicks over the side of the nest, I could tell exactly when it had happened because of the behaviour of the parents. The tenderness they showed to their newborn chicks was incredible. I remember the way that the father, when the mother had gone out to feed herself, had been left in charge of the nest. He stepped so carefully, with feet bigger than my stretched-out hand, so as not to hurt the chicks. I could tell he was just waiting for the female to come back so he could resume his usual hunting duties, trying desperately not to damage the chicks in the meantime. He and his partner are examples of the largest bird of prey in the UK, with a wingspan of around 2.5 metres (8 feet) and a weight of 6.5 kilograms (14 pounds). They are also some of the rarest birds in the country as they became extinct about 100 years ago due to poaching and had to be reintroduced from Norway. They are making a comeback, but there are still only around 150 pairs.

Then there was the first moment I saw the chicks, finally big enough so that their heads were visible over the edge of the nest. Two chicks – one female and one male – with tiny, fragile, white, fluffy bodies, always calling for their mother.

The father would do most of the hunting while the mother stood guard on her perch, watching the nest with her beady eyes – a little like what I was doing from the other side. Watching her chicks through my lens. I became familiar with the signs that the father was coming back with a meal – I learned the way that the chicks behaved a few seconds before he dropped the fish. I could then make sure the camera was rolling as he flew in. I knew, also, that the mother would then arrive to feed the chicks. She would give the lion's share to whoever begged the most – which happened to be the female – who grew much bigger and stronger than her brother.

I've watched them grow day by day. I've seen the parents do their duty through night and day. I've watched their feathers slowly turn from white to brown, losing their downy newborn layer. I know their calls and what they mean. I understand what their body language says. I know these birds like they are my own children.

My rhythm has become in tune with theirs. Every day I get up before dawn and pack my 35 kilos (77 pounds) of equipment to take up the hill. It takes more than an hour to walk the 3 kilometres (2 miles) with that amount of stuff.

At the beginning I would do it all myself, trudging up the hill toward the nest, wondering why I ever signed up for this. Thankfully, one rainy day when I'd decided not to film, I was chatting with my neighbour Jonny, complaining about all my aches and pains and about what an effort it was to get up to the hide, and he said, "Hey, Hamza, I'll help you with your things." When I found out he was in that TV show Gladiators many years ago, I knew he was a keeper! Every day since then he has helped me carry my bags up the hill and then comes back as it gets dark to help me down again.

That's the great thing about life in rural Scotland – people are neighbourly and kind. It really reminds me of where I grew up in Sudan, Northeast Africa, in a small community. If you need help with anything, there will always be someone there for you. So I accepted Jonny's offer to take half the weight for me, trusting that I would, at some point, help someone out with similar generosity.

The eagles have grown accustomed to our routine. They have their own routine to match it. As we approach, the adult on duty – usually the mother – alarm calls, then flies to a perch from which she can watch us. I carefully climb inside the camouflage hide and get my stuff set up, whisper a thanks and goodbye to Jonny, and he leaves quietly. I change out of my sweaty clothes into something dry. I learned that the hard way after spending the first day shivering in my cold sweat.

Once Jonny leaves, the adult flies back to the nest and looks right down the camera lens as if to say, "Yep, we know you are there, black man. We know your white friend has left but that you will be staying. As long as you are in the hide, we are all okay." I feel, in a strange way, somewhat accepted. It makes me feel so connected to these birds, so alive. Just as I was accepted into the Ardnamurchan community, I have also been accepted by this family of eagles.

Once I'm established in my hillside hide, the rest of my day is spent sitting and watching the nest. I'm usually covered in ticks and midges but I don't dare move too much in case I disturb the eagles. The last thing I would want is for them to get freaked and move somewhere else. It took me four years to get my licence from NatureScot to get close to the eagles; I had to prove that I was not just anyone – I was a professional with important footage to capture – and that I knew what I was doing. It took several years to build up a good enough portfolio to grant a licence. If I scared the eagles and caused them to move, my reputation would be damaged and I would never get this licence back.

At the end of each day, after about 12 hours of sitting and watching the nest, turning on the camera for any interesting events, Jonny comes to pick me up. I'm always so grateful to see him, to be able to communicate with another human. On the way down the hill, I tell him stories about the eagles. He shares news about what's been happening in the village. As we approach, people pop out of their houses and ask, "Did they fledge yet? What happened today?" This community is invested and they want to know the story of the eagles. It is such an honour to be able to connect them with their avian neighbours in a stronger way.

Eventually, after filling everyone in on the events of the day, I get home, plug in my camera batteries to charge, start the download of my day's footage, make myself a quick dinner, take a shower and roll into bed. I get a couple of hours' sleep before my alarm rudely awakens me to signify it's time to pack my things and meet Jonny for another round with the eagles.

This has been my life for eight weeks and it's exhausting.

Now all I need is to capture this young chick fledging and my task is done. The stakes are feeling very, very high.

Six days ago I'd taken a quarter of an hour longer than usual to climb up to the hide. Jonny was encouraging me to keep going but I felt like I could just sit down on the spot and pass out. I'd lost almost 13 kilograms (28 pounds) since the beginning of the shoot from climbing the hill day in, day out, and my body and eyes were tired. I was so ready for the chicks to fledge. The female chick had spent the previous few days holding onto a branch on the outside of the nest, flapping but not opening her talons. I kept praying please, please, just open them.

When we arrived at the nest that morning, just that tiny bit late, I did my usual sweep of the nest to check they were both there. I couldn't believe it. The larger, female chick had gone. She'd already fledged! Without me! A wave of anger and disappointment overtook me, and I felt like crying and screaming. I felt almost betrayed by her, as if she knew my intention and had deliberately chosen to go when I wasn't watching. It must have been within the last half hour, as the light had only just broken.

That's the thing about nature, I guess, things happen when they are ready – nothing waits for you. Despite the disappointment, I accepted what had happened and resolved not to miss the fledging of the second chick. Capturing this footage would be instrumental in building the career I'd been striving for.

––––––––––

Let's rewind back to nine years ago, the time I decided to make Scotland my home, to be surrounded by this incredible wildlife permanently. I had finished my masters degree in biological imaging and photography, after completing a zoology with conservation and animal behaviour degree at Bangor University, and I knew I wanted to pursue wildlife filmmaking. I just didn't know how to start. During the summer, a friend on the course took me with him to visit the Ardnamurchan peninsula. I was stunned by the landscape and the wildlife, the rugged mountains, the bright green grass, the white beaches and the clean sea air. Just across the water, a small boat ride away, there are islands of puffins and other sea birds. There are seals and porpoises, dolphins and basking sharks passing right off the shore. Otters scamper around the bays and pine martins scurry across people's back decks. There are majestic red deer on the hillsides, among the flowering heather and gorse. There are more types of bird of prey here than anywhere else I had been in the UK.

I knew straight away that it was the place for me. If I couldn't make it as a wildlife photographer on the Ardnamurchan peninsular, I wasn't going to make it anywhere.

So two weeks later I moved up. I had my camera kit, a few clothes, a sleeping bag and a pillow. Most importantly I had a car, which became my home for six months. Every morning I would wake up in the Ardnamurchan ferry terminal car park and think I was the luckiest man alive. I was so happy to be surrounded by this beautiful landscape.

I did all sorts of jobs at the beginning, just trying to earn enough to rent a place. I worked as a gillie – the Scots word for "manservant" – stalking and managing deer herds and guiding visitors around the rugged landscapes; I cut grass and chopped logs for elderly people. In the meantime I was doing my own photography, and applying for bursary after bursary. I got many rejections but I kept going, never giving up.

It was tough – but what kept me going was that I knew, if anything went wrong, I had amazingly supportive parents who would catch my fall. In the past, if I'd needed somewhere to stay or some financial support, my parents would always offer their help, without conditions. My parents' support made me confident enough to take risks.

Was this little chick going to be brave like I was? Would he trust his parents to catch his fall? I just had to watch and wait.

After many hours of coaxing, the female senses that the male chick isn't going to fledge. I've been watching him, non-stop, through the camera, and I feel as impatient as she does. My body is stiff and my back aches from being in the same position for far too long. So far he hasn't even shown any desire to move toward her. Unlike the female chick, he hasn't moved onto the outer branches to practise his flapping; he hasn't even explored the edge of the nest. He has stayed, rooted to the spot, calling for his mother to bring him the fish she has ready. Please, I whisper, please let it be today; I can't do this anymore. Although I realize that it's getting late and it would be silly for him to fledge at this point in the day. Birds usually fledge in the mornings when there are fewer predators about on the forest floor, in case they fall and injure themselves.

The mother finally gives up and flies over. She drops the fish into the nest for him, ruffles her feathers sulkily, then takes off and returns to her perch. So I guess the lucky chap isn't going to fledge tonight then – there's no longer an incentive. He starts tucking into the mackerel, pulling off flakes of flesh. Just as he puts his head down for a second bite, I see something in the corner of the lens. It's a flash of a wing from another family member – has the mother come back? Why?

I soon realize it's his sister that's back in the nest – very interesting! I hit the record button and hold my breath. I can't imagine why she's back; she had already fledged.

Talons out, she begins to hammer the back of his head while he's eating the fish. She must be hungry, having been using energy to fly all day, probably having little luck with hunting. She's jealous – he's still getting special treatment from their mother.

The male chick isn't strong enough to fight back – she's much bigger than him. So he submits to her, lowering his body, squawking, and not looking at her.

She leans over and picks at the fish from beside him, taking her time to eat every last mouthful. He continues squawking and looking down.

She finishes off the fish. I'm expecting her to stretch her wings and fly off indignantly. But no, it seems her vendetta toward her brother is stronger than that. She squares up to him, as if to say, "Right, that's it – if you're not going to fledge I'm going to do it for you. I'm not going to watch you get all the food, you little mummy's boy." She lashes out with her talons in front of her, pushing him. Finally retaliating, he picks up his talons to meet her – they push each other with their feet, wings flapping behind. I'm rooting for the little chap – come on, show her what you are made of!

But she's that much stronger, having eaten the lion's share of their food growing up. She was the greedy favourite, not him. He loses strength, drops his talons and bows his head, defeated. With that, she takes hold of his chest in her talons and gives him a final push toward the edge of the nest. He doesn't retaliate as she moves in and boots him out.

That's it. He's gone. He hasn't fledged but he's certainly not in the nest. I peer closer, my heart in my mouth. I realize he's underneath the nest, grabbing onto a branch. Will he be able to save himself? Is he hurt? Did she puncture his chest with her talons?

And then he falls – all the way down to the bottom of the tree.

Oh no, I whisper under my breath. Surely he will now fall prey to some wild animals as it's getting dark. He's vulnerable.

His sister is still on the nest, fluffing up her feathers proudly. Then she spreads her wings and takes off.

The nest is empty.

I can't believe it. My task is complete. But what an ending. I can't celebrate the fledge as I'd expected. I can't believe that she pushed him out of the nest. How insane!

I carefully climb out of the tent, stretching my legs and arms. I feel lightheaded as I stand up for the first time in many hours, but I can't just sit there with the nest empty, not knowing if the little fella is dead or alive. I have to climb down.

It's slippery and dangerous, but I manage to support myself holding onto tree branches, and carefully lower myself down the steep slope so that I can see the bottom of the tree.

He is there, and he's very much alive. He doesn't appear to be bleeding. He's calling for his mother. She calls back to him, reassuringly. "I am here," she seems to say. "I saw what she did to you." I get a sudden flurry of anxiety. What should I do? Do I need to call for help? I can hardly allow one of the rarest birds of prey in the UK to get eaten by a fox but is it ethical to intervene? How could I even help?

I get out my phone and search through my contacts. I find David, the eagle officer at the RSPB. He'll know what to do.

"There's nothing you can do," David tells me. "He'll just have to fledge from there if he's not taken first."

I gulp.

"Taken? You mean, like, eaten?"

"Yes, that could happen. That's just life, isn't it? You could do more damage by capturing him. There's a lot to all of that – captivity, release … you know. It's much better he finds his own way."

As it turned out, he fledged from the ground two days later. I went back for those two days, to watch and record it. I wanted to see the outcome, even if it was bad. So did the community, so did my parents – we had all been following the progress of this chick for months and we couldn't give up on him.

For those two days the parents each took responsibility for one of the chicks. The father took the young female off the territory, presumably to hunt, and the mother kept feeding the male – taking the fish to him on the forest floor before resuming her watch high in the trees.

Luckily no unwelcome predators came hunting in those two days. They may have tried during the night but, if they did, the mother didn't let them anywhere near her chick.

I couldn't help feeling some sense of familiarity with that young male. I remember what it was like moving from northern Sudan to the UK, aged eight. I was totally out of my depth, like being on the forest floor, vulnerable and confused. What was this strange place? What were they saying to me? Why weren't we allowed to go outside in the rain? In Sudan we would just dry off in 2 minutes after being caught in the rain, but it was different here. I felt overwhelmed by how different it was, how cold it was, but I just had to deal with it.

Jacob was allocated as my buddy at school. I remember the first time we were introduced I was amazed at his long, blonde hair and blue eyes. I thought he must have coloured in his eyes with crayons! I tried calling him "Yaqub", his name in my mother tongue so as to show some sort of familiarity, but he told me no, it was "Jayycobb".

I had to learn to fly from the ground when all the other children in my class were a level up – knowing the culture and the language.

They knew what fountain pens were – and no, they didn't spurt out water! They knew that Father Christmas didn't have a son. How strange, a father without a son, I thought. I had to quickly adapt to a new culture, learn a language, and I was exposed to a new god (he did have a son, which was something new).

––––––––––

The young male chick also did things differently, unlike what was expected by his family – just like me. I come from a long line of doctors and dentists. Both my older siblings trained at medical school, much to my parents' delight. I was never that academic, and I often felt like the failure in the family. In fact, I have dyslexia, so struggled through all of my exams.

I always loved wildlife and being in nature. I couldn't imagine myself in a white coat, indoors all day, working with people. I deeply respect my siblings' profession, but I could never relate to it. I always felt like the outsider in the family.

So I wasn't the strongest or the most academic – I didn't follow the typical path – but my parents always supported me. Just like these white-tailed eagles, my parents adapted their expectations and were always encouraging. I often call them after a shoot and share my good news with them. My mother always tells me how proud she is of me. Deep down, I think they like it that I do things differently.

That young female, though, she's a lot meaner than my siblings! I pondered on her behaviour for quite a while after watching her push the male out of the nest. Why did she do that? Was she just greedy? Jealous? I supposed it was survival of the fittest in action – but really – trying to kill off your own brother?

I aired some of my thoughts to Jonny as we walked down the hill on the final day, feeling a sense of deep relief that the job was done – but tender, too.

"People can be greedy, too," said Jonny. "Did you see the news recently? There's no toilet paper left in any of the stores.

It's a bloody flu-like virus, not food poisoning! What are people playing at?"

"Yes," I agreed. "What about old people and those who go late to the stores? What are they going to do? Hoarding is so unnecessary – people should just take what they need."

"I guess we humans have a bit of a hangover from our hunter-gatherer past, when things were scarce and we would need to consume a lot at once," said Jonny.

"Yes, but we're not hunter-gatherers now," I responded. And if we were, I'm sure we'd use our resources better and have a better relationship with other species. We would know the importance of sharing for everyone's benefit."

Personally, when I think about what we have done as humans, how we have treated other animals, plants and insects, I feel saddened. We humans think this planet is ours and ours alone. It is not. Through my work I try to show people that there are other species important to our ecosystem, amazing creatures that are worth sharing with.

In my home I don't turn out the pine martens from the attic, or the birds from the eaves in the roof – they were there first. My home is also their home, and this planet is also their planet. I strongly believe that we need to learn to share better with other creatures if we are going to have any chance of creating a better world. Just like the eagles had shared their space with me.

So it had been a tough but fascinating summer with the white-tailed eagles. I felt humbled to have spent those precious moments with them. They had become like my family, and I felt accepted by them into their world.

My hard work paid off and I was recognized for my efforts. The BBC used some of my footage in a documentary they made about my life in Scotland, a camera operator living a wild and remote life. The story of the eagles was shared with thousands of the British public. I finally made myself, and my family, very proud.

CHARACTERISTICS OF LIFE

CAMILLE DUNGY

Ask me if I speak for the snail and I will tell you
I speak for the snail.
speak of underneathedness
and the welcome of mosses,
of life that springs up,
little lives that pull back and wait for a moment.

I speak for the damselfly, water skeet, mollusk,
the caterpillar, the beetle, the spider, the ant.
I speak
from the time before spinelessness was frowned upon.

Ask me if I speak for the moon jelly. I will tell you
one thing today and another tomorrow
and I will be as consistent as anything alive
on this earth.

I move as the currents move, with the breezes.
What part of your nature drives you? You, in your cubicle
ought to understand me. I filter and filter and filter all day.

Ask me if I speak for the nautilus and I will be silent
as the nautilus shell on a shelf. I can be beautiful
and useless if that's all you know to ask of me.

Ask me what I know of longing and I will speak of distances
between meadows of night-blooming flowers.
I will speak
the impossible hope of the firefly.

You with the candle
burning and only one chair at your table must understand
such wordless desire.

To say it is mindless is missing the point.

From *Characteristics of Life*, Trophic Cascade © 2017
by Camille Dungy. Published by Wesleyan
University Press. Used by permission.

Camille is a poet from the USA, having authored four
collections including *Trophic Cascade* (2017). She was
a 2019 Guggenheim Fellow and is a Distinguished
Professor at Colorado State University.

After working in London for 11 years as management consultant, Roz wanted to seek a life richer in meaning and purpose. An environmental awakening in 2003 inspired her to row, solo, across three oceans, using her voyages as a campaigning platform to raise awareness of our ecological crises. She holds four Guinness World Records for ocean rowing, and was voted National Geographic Adventurer of the Year in 2010.

This is an insight into what being alone on a vast ocean meant for her.

ONE OAR STROKE AT A TIME

ROZ SAVAGE

It was 2009 and I was rowing across the Pacific Ocean, alone. As you can probably imagine, this was taking a while.

If you haven't come across the rather obscure and masochistic sport of ocean rowing, I may need to offer a few words of explanation. The objective is to row across several thousand miles of ocean – and most people start, as I did, with the Atlantic, it being the narrowest of the major bodies of salt water – totally independently. The ocean rower takes all the food, medical supplies and tools that they will need for months at sea, and an onboard desalinator-watermaker purifies fresh drinking water from seawater. Most ocean rowers join a crew of two, four or even more rowers. A few of us decide to take the masochism up a notch by going solo. There is no support boat, no chase vessel. A satellite phone provides a slender (and expensive) umbilical cord to shore, but that is the only interpersonal communication.

I had been a latecomer to the life of adventure. After obtaining a law degree from Oxford, I worked as a management consultant before an early mid-life crisis combined with an environmental epiphany led me to set my sights on rowing across three oceans, using my adventures to raise awareness of our ecological challenges via the resulting blog posts, social media, talks and books.

By 2009 I had already soloed the Atlantic during the stormiest-ever transatlantic season, had one failed attempt on the Pacific – aborted due to rough conditions and equipment failures – and had successfully rowed the first stage of the Pacific, from San Francisco to Hawaii.

The trans-Pacific voyage would end up taking a total of eight months, split into three stages. I was now rowing the second of the three stages, from Hawaii to the Republic of Kiribati, a leg that would take me across the International Date Line and across the equator, from the westernmost part of the northern hemisphere into the easternmost part of the southern hemisphere.

At the time of this story, I was rowing through the doldrums, the equatorial region when the wind drops to nothing, the sun beats down and it feels hot enough to boil your brains. The day had been sweltering. The night was a little cooler, but it was still airless and stifling in the sleeping cabin. It was an unusually calm night, a welcome respite from the usual relentless pitching and yawing of the boat, so I decided to lie out on the deck for a while – at least until the next rain squall came along. I dragged my sleeping bag out of the cabin and snuggled down between the runners of the rowing seat.

As my boat rocked gently on the swell, I found myself suddenly marvelling at the strangeness and splendour of my life. It was as if I rose up outside myself for a moment and looked down at this little naked woman lying on the deck of her tiny silver rowboat, completely alone in the vast darkness of the ocean.

Who would have thought, ten years previously when I was still working in an office in London, doing a job I didn't like to buy stuff I didn't need, that one day I would find myself here, in the middle of the Pacific, well on my way to becoming the first woman to row across the world's largest ocean? There had been some scary moments that had tested me almost beyond my limits, but they had also helped me become stronger, to form a character that could withstand the challenges of life – not just on the ocean, but on dry land too. I thought back to that unhappy, underachieving management consultant who had dragged herself into the office every day because she thought she had no choice. I was immensely happy that I had reached that fork in the road, and that I had chosen the road – or ocean – less travelled.

I snuggled in deeper and gazed up at the stars dotting the inky darkness above. Thousands of miles from light pollution, the night sky was stunning. The stars glittered across the night sky like a jewel-encrusted cape, the Milky Way a sparkling sash. The longer I looked, the more stars I saw, until it seemed as if the entire sky was studded with diamonds.

As I lay there, I imagined the planets and moons orbiting all those stars, and for a precious moment I forgot everything. I forgot about my blisters, my heat rash and my aching shoulders. I forgot my nationality and my gender and the colour of my skin. I forgot who I was and where I was, and why. I even forgot to be human, and simply allowed myself to be absorbed into the spellbinding beauty of the night sky. For a brief, incredible moment, I transcended my puny existence, feeling as tiny and insignificant as a mote of dust but at the same time at one with the infinite majesty of the universe. I was everything, and everything was me. I was everywhere, and nowhere. I knew everything, and I knew nothing. I was intensely present, and I was eternal. I was just a tiny speck of consciousness, and yet I was consciousness itself, omnipresent and omnipotent. I was suddenly overcome with a profound sense of joy.

Then a squall blew in and I had to scurry back to the cabin, but the magic of that moment has stayed with me ever since. Compared with the vastness of the universe, our planet is tiny, our lives fleeting. In a sense, none of it matters.

And yet, all of it matters. This earth is a miracle, the culmination of an elegant evolutionary process that has generated an incredible diversity of spectacular life forms, including us.

To each of us, our lives matter. And I believe that to the earth, even to the universe, we matter too.

It took me around 3 million oar strokes to cross the Pacific. One oar stroke didn't propel me very far – maybe just a metre or two. And yet every oar stroke was necessary to get me from one side of the ocean to the other. Every oar stroke mattered; it got me a fraction closer to my destination. And even more importantly, each oar stroke told me a story about who I am. Every single one told me I am someone who is strong, persevering, determined. I am someone who can be brave, resourceful, tenacious. As oar stroke accumulated upon oar stroke, it reinforced again and again this story about myself.

And likewise, every single thing I do, or you do, or anybody does, contributes to the future we are creating together. It contributes to the story of humanity. I believe that in a very real sense, everything we think, say and do makes a difference, no matter how infinitesimally small, to the universe we inhabit, and we do a great disservice to ourselves and to our world if we disown that responsibility and that privilege.

Never believe that you are too small to make a difference. We are all making a difference, all the time. Is yours going to be the right kind of difference?

SEA CHANTS

BY SELINA TUSITALA MARSH

when I'm broken ~~

I go to the sea ~~ when I'm open ~~

I go to the sea ~~ when I can't let hope in ~~

I go to the sea ~~ when hope comes in ~~ *I go to the sea* ~~

when I live lies ~~ *I go to the sea* ~~ when I am wise ~~ *I go to the sea* ~~ when I die ~~

I go to the sea ~~ when I rise ~~ *I go to the sea* ~~

when I'm lonely ~~ *I go to the sea* ~~

when I'm alone ~~

I go to the sea ~~

when I am lost ~~ *I go to the sea* ~~

when I am home ~~ *I go to the sea* ~~ when I escape ~~

I go to the sea ~~ when I debate ~~ *I go to the sea* ~~ when I'm afraid ~~

I go to the sea ~~ when I am brave ~~ *I go to the sea* ~~ when I need freedom ~~

I go to the sea ~~ when I am free ~~ *I go to the sea* ~~ when I need me ~~ *I go to the sea* ~~

when I am me ~~ *I go to the sea* ~~ when I need rest ~~ *I go to the sea* ~~

when I confess ~~ *I go to the sea* ~~ when it's too much ~~

I go to the sea ~~ when it's enough ~~

I go to the sea ~~

when I want more ~~
I go to the sea ~~ when less is more ~~
I go to the sea ~~ when I'm unsure ~~ *I go to the sea* ~~
when I'm so sure ~~ *I go to the sea* ~~ when I mourn mum ~~ *I go to the sea* ~~
when I adorn mum ~~ *I go to the sea* ~~ when I can't feel ~~
I go to the sea ~~ when it's too real ~~
I go to the sea ~~

when I need healing ~~
I go to the sea ~~ when I reveal ~~
I go to the sea ~~ when I'm disconnected ~~
I go to the sea ~~ when I'm reconnected ~~ *I go to the sea* ~~
when I'm rejected ~~ *I go to the sea* ~~ when I'm selected ~~ *I go to the sea* ~~
when I can't find heart ~~ *I go to the sea* ~~ when I start with heart ~~
I go to the sea ~~ when nothing lasts ~~ *I go to the sea* ~~
~~ in infinity ~~ *I go to the sea* ~~
~~ when I doubt my worth ~~
~~ *I go to the sea* ~~
when I know it ~~

I go to the sea ~~ when I eat earth ~~
I go to the sea ~~ when I sow it ~~ *I go to the sea* ~~
when I don't try ~~ *I go to the sea* ~~ when I've tried it all ~~ *I go to the sea* ~~
when I don't know why ~~ *I go to the sea* ~~ when I know why ~~ *I go to the sea* ~~
when I am unseen ~~ *I go to the sea* ~~ when I am seen ~~ *I go to the sea* ~~
when I cleave ~~ *I go to the sea* ~~ when I believe ~~ *I go to the sea* ~~
when incomplete ~~ *I go to the sea* ~~ when I'm whole ~~
I go to the sea ~~ when I wage war ~~ *I go to the sea* ~~
when I ignore ~~ *I go to the sea* ~~
when I am bound ~~

I go to the sea ~~
when I am free ~~ I go to the sea ~~
when I seek ground ~~ I go to the sea ~~ when I am a tree ~~
I go to the sea ~~ when I'm heavy ~~ I go to the sea ~~ when I am light ~~
I go to the sea ~~ when I'm unsteady ~~ I go to the sea ~~ when I am set right ~~
I go to the sea ~~ when I need to be ~~ I go to the sea ~~ when I am ~~
I go to the sea ~~ when I flee ~~ I go to the sea ~~ when I stand ~~
I go to the sea ~~ when I don't understand ~~ I go to the sea ~~
when I expand ~~ I go to the sea ~~ when I need a plan ~~
I go to the sea ~~ when I plan ~~ I go to the sea ~~
when I'm ashamed ~~ I go to the sea ~~
when I'm steady-eyed ~~

I go to the sea ~~
when I should have stayed ~~ I go to the sea ~~
when I stay with pride ~~ I go to the sea ~~ when I should have left ~~
I go to the sea ~~ when I go ~~ I go to the sea ~~ when I am bereft ~~ I go to the sea ~~
when I am blessed ~~ I go to the sea ~~ when I should've asked ~~
I go to the sea ~~ when I ask ~~ I go to the sea ~~
when I can't last ~~ I go to the sea ~~
when I last ~~ I go to the sea ~~
when I need to cry ~~

I go to the sea ~~
when I cry ~~ I go to the sea ~~
when I don't know why ~~ I go to the sea ~~ when I know my why ~~
I go to the sea ~~ when I should've known ~~ I go to the sea ~~ when I know ~~
I go to the sea ~~ when I feel alone ~~ I go to the sea ~~ when I am home ~~
I go to the sea ~~ when no one shows ~~ I go to the sea ~~
when everyone's there ~~ I go to the sea ~~
when nothing grows ~~
I go to the sea ~~
when I pray ~~

I go to the sea ~~

when I am split ~~ *I go to the sea* ~~

when I am knit ~~ *I go to the sea* ~~ when I don't church it ~~

I go to the sea ~~ when I worship ~~ *I go to the sea* ~~ when I need time ~~

I go to the sea ~~ when I make time ~~ *I go to the sea* ~~ when I need mine ~~ *I go to the sea* ~~

when I have mine ~~ *I go to the sea* ~~ when I don't want this ~~ *I go to the sea* ~~

when I want this ~~ *I go to the sea* ~~ when I'm not his ~~ *I go to the sea* ~~

when I am his ~~ *I go to the sea* ~~ when I'm not free ~~

I go to the sea ~~ when I am free ~~ *I go to the sea* ~~

when I can't see ~~ *I go to the sea* ~~ when I see ~~

I go to the sea ~~ *I go to the sea* ~~

I go to the ~~

I go to ~~

I go ~~

I ~~

Sea Chants © Selina Tusitala Marsh, 2023

Selina represented Tuvalu in the Poetry Olympics in
London 2012, was named the official Commonwealth
poet in 2016, and was appointed to the position of
New Zealand Poet Laureate 2017–19.

Gregory was homeless for much of his adult life. Aged 35, he turned his back on society and became a hermit, living alone on a mountaintop in eastern Australia. After ten years in exile, he walked out of the wilderness in 1999 to face the challenge of resuming civilized life using some of the wisdom gained in the forest. He is now a lecturer in sociology at Southern Cross University, as well as a tireless advocate for homeless and disaffected people.

This story explores his physical and emotional journey in the forest.

FINDING OF SELF IN A FOREST: LESSONS FOR LATER

GREGORY P SMITH

It rained hard on the day I went to live in the forest: fitting weather for a life that had felt like an endless storm. In her wisdom, Mother Nature decided the drenching alone wasn't enough; she sent me a welcoming party of blood-sucking parasites, too.

I'd been born into violence. The chaotic corridors of my abusive family home gave way to more regimented forms of assault and cruelty at the Catholic orphanage where my parents abandoned me at the age of ten. Little wonder I became a runaway and, after that, a juvenile inmate. Set loose on the world at 19 with precious little schooling, I endured long, troubled years on the streets, almost entirely disengaged from society.

What should have been the prime of my life passed in a blur of meaningless wanderings up and down Australia's eastern seaboard. I took menial jobs where I could, scavenged for food and slept wherever I found a dry space in which to curl into a ball. Although I loathed and resented society – after all, society hadn't the slightest regard for me – I directed my most searing hatred inward. I was disgusted with myself and deeply ashamed about who I was.

Preferring the security of an emotional fortress, I locked all of humanity out of my miserable little world – even my younger sisters who'd suffered alongside me at home and in the orphanage. I became a violent, menacing, erratic and often drunken misfit. As much as I put fear into others, though, the truth is I was terrified of them. I was terrified of everyone. I'd had too many bad experiences with human beings to even begin to trust them, so I avoided them at all costs.

It's not really surprising that I felt strangely safe crouching in the forest, alone in failing light and the driving rain.

I'd wandered in there on a whim late one afternoon some time in 1989. The towering eucalyptus trees and native palms formed a cool, quiet living cathedral atop a small mountain range in the subtropical hinterland of the New South Wales north coast. I'd found it, quite literally, at the end of the road during one of my long walks to nowhere.

I had with me the worldly possessions I'd amassed in my 35 years on the planet: army boots and the clothes I was wearing, a Driza-Bone raincoat and a backpack containing semi-useful knick-knacks and comforts – a pocket knife, a box of matches, a candle, tobacco, marijuana, some nuts, a short piece of rope, some cheap wine …

Exhausted and miserable, but relieved to be alone, I squatted on the sodden earth and pulled the coat over my head while fat raindrops drummed hard on my back. As darkness fell, I became aware that 10 or 12 leeches had taken up residence on my lower legs. In the gloaming they looked like little blood-filled cocoons attached to pale, skinny branches.

The leeches had the decency to inject me with anaesthetic so I didn't feel any pain, and I decided to let them feed for a while. I figured it was a fair price to pay. After all, I'd arrived on their doorstep unannounced so they were only returning the favour. Oddly, it also felt as if I'd entered into a contract with the wild – a bodily exchange between the forest and I.

Dawn broke, clear and pale blue. I found a small pool of sunlight to warm myself in and dry out a little. If I'd felt secure but sorry for myself the previous night, the morning brought a feeling of enchantment. The sun's increasing wattage turned the vegetation from pre-dawn grey into every shade of green on the spectrum. Broad-leaved undergrowth covered the undulating terrain while elegant gum-trees reached languidly into the sapphire sky. The air smelled sweet, thick blankets of lichen and moss were draped over colossal fallen trees and birdsong drifted down from the leafy canopy high above.

Over the next few days, I plunged deeper and deeper into the forest's embrace. It wasn't long before I started to ponder whether it might become my home – my first permanent abode since childhood.

Storm clouds regularly dragged their waterlogged bellies over the mountaintop, and it became clear if I was going to stay in the forest I'd need to find a place with good drainage (I learned later it was, in fact, a rainforest). Eventually I came across a promising looking gully, split by a fern-fringed creek that gurgled over moss-coated rocks. I followed the water west and watched it plunge over the edge of a 100-metre (328-foot) cliff into a richly forested valley below.

The 180-degree view from the top of the waterfall was awe-inspiring. The valley opened wide to the south and the distant cliff face on the opposite side was painted with the streaking white spray of half a dozen high waterfalls. It was there, after smoking a joint and eating a pawpaw, that I decided I'd probably never leave.

On either side of the waterfall, the clifftops climbed at a gradient of about 30 degrees. After exploring the bluff on the south side, I found a small clearing on a large, sloping bed of lava rock. It looked like it would drain easily when storms swept in and it was well away from the main trail that led into the forest and, thus, any humans who might enter.

At first I was mostly only aware of the birdlife and the occasional lizard I'd spy out of the corner of my eye. The sound of movement in the undergrowth spooked me to begin with, but once my senses tuned in to the natural world my life started to mesh with the other creatures that lived there.

A favourite discovery in the early days of my hermit kingdom was a vivid blue crayfish that lived in a deep rock pool down by the creek. The water was so clear that the majestic crustacean looked like a display under museum glass. I was so taken with the idea that a shimmering lobster-like creature could make its home on a mountaintop that it eventually became a strong spiritual symbol. Like me, the crayfish had taken refuge from the world and it seemed content in its solitude. We were soulmates. No matter how hungry I would get, I could never bring myself to kill and eat it. I couldn't say the same about my other neighbours.

Fire also took on a hugely important role in my new life. While in the past I only used it to light cigarettes, I gained an appreciation of its crucial role since the beginning of humanity. Aside from its value for warmth, cooking and morale, fire became spiritually important to me, too. Hours, days – even weeks – could drift by in meditations as I sat hypnotized by the ballet of flames.

For the first year or so, my camp was nothing more than a circle of stones around the fire, two larger rocks I'd arranged into a seat and a table-cum-workspace, and a bed. My mattress was simply a stack of giant fern leaves, harvested from other gullies at least half an hour's walk away and placed on the lava rock. For all the fireside contemplation, I always circled back to destructive thoughts, painful memories and a deepening shame about the appalling state of my life.

I was anxious not to create any kind of footprint in my immediate environment, lest I give my existence away to anyone else who might venture into my realm. I took the same approach with firewood as I did when harvesting ferns. I never pulled sticks off trees and instead relied on dead-fall branches, also collected from further afield.

Smoke posed another security consideration. I quickly learned that if wood was even slightly green it emitted white plumes when burned. Putting it on the fire during daylight hours was akin to dropping a pin on Google Maps. Only super-dead, super-dry branches would do during the day, but at night I could risk slipping some greener wood into the mix: the resultant smoke also helped keep the ever-present mosquitoes under control.

Thankfully I didn't have to share my camp with the leeches (my well-chosen campsite was too dry), but I did have to contend with some other fairly annoying roommates. Ants, spiders and flies were a permanent nuisance, like the mosquitoes. Ticks caused me plenty of problems, too, particularly when they burrowed into the middle of my back, out of reach of my searching fingers. On those occasions I had to rub my spine against a tree like some homeless grizzly bear.

Every few months I'd walk for two days to one of the towns nearer the coast (usually at night to avoid those pesky humans as much as possible) and buy some basic comforts like powdered milk, rice and – most importantly – matches. Once restocked, I'd scurry back to my sanctuary on the shoulder of the waterfall.

In the beginning forest life was kind of fun. Roaming around semi-naked and learning to survive in the wild made me feel like the supreme ruler of a universe of one. I could do whatever I wanted, whenever I wanted. I'd lie on my back in the fast-running flows at the top of the waterfall for hours and watch the birds go about their day. I'd launch exploratory missions to all corners of the mountaintop, studiously avoiding other people who sometimes wandered along the main trail. I could never outrun hunger, though. Most of the time I was thinking about what I could eat next.

Contrary to popular belief, food is hard to find in a forest. This is especially true if you stay in one place for a long time. After a while you run out of things to eat. Now and then I'd liberate fruit – mostly pawpaw and avocados – from the private orchards or farms on the outskirts of the forest, but when it came to protein I'd catch and kill my own.

Since I was the apex predator, I thought nothing was off the menu. I ate everything – from worms and grubs I'd find in the silt under rocks near the creek, to small marsupials and reptiles I'd trap using simple snares. I even caught a large diamond python when I woke in terror one night to find it inching across my chest.

I skinned the snake the following day and cooked the meat on skewers dangled over the coals. That night, and for weeks afterwards, I was haunted by terrible recurring nightmares about serpents and demons stabbing and burning me in a fire. It rattled me badly and I tried to calm myself, rationalizing that snakes were "taboo" food for me and that Mother Nature was just teaching me a lesson. The episode made me understand her providence was not unconditional: I couldn't simply help myself to anything I pleased. Eating the wrong thing could easily poison my body or, in the case of the diamond python, toxify my dreams. Thankfully the nightmares gradually subsided and snakes joined the crayfish on my protected species list.

It followed that the more I killed the local wildlife, the less of it there was. After a year or so, most of the smaller marsupials in my little gully were gone. There were no kangaroos, wallabies, or other large prey around. Fortunately, I found a colony of bats in a stand of trees not too far from camp. I fashioned a sling using a piece of cloth torn from a T-shirt and became adept at knocking bats off their lofty perches with rocks. After seizing the stunned mammals on the forest floor, I'd break their necks, wrap them in their leathery wings and roast them on the coals. I became so proficient with stone and sling that bats were my main source of protein for a few years.

Eventually, though, I stopped killing animals altogether. I knew I could survive without other creatures having to suffer in the process. I could eat fruit, vegetables, and even eggs pilfered from surrounding orchards and farms: I could procure rice and flour during quick resupply missions to the towns, and I could scavenge for food at night in dumpsters behind cafés and bakeries. This dietary conversion was driven by the deep reverence I'd developed for nature. I had become part of the natural world and the affinity caused me to feel sharp regret over my predation in the forest. Without understanding the consequences of abruptly eliminating protein from my diet, I became a strict vegetarian.

Over time, I also amassed more possessions at the campsite.

Bottles and jars were used for storing food and other perishables. I had a tarpaulin for shelter for a while, too, after the Driza-Bone raincoat eventually rotted and fell to pieces. I even bought a set of glass marbles at a hippy marketplace and kept them with me at all times. My oh-so-funny in-joke was, "Well, at least I haven't lost my marbles!" But there were times I wasn't so sure about that.

Despite this modest estate in the bush, I spent most of my time focusing on other stuff I'd dragged in there with me – namely my colossal and confronting pile of emotional baggage. I'd slump by the fire, drunk and stoned, and unpack the ugly past. I'd sift through the mental files and try to understand why society hated me so, how I'd ended up a hermit and why I had no one to love or be loved by.

I injured myself plenty of times as I rambled across the mountaintop year after year. I'd suffered deep cuts, burns, bruises, sprains, fractures and any number of bites and stings but the worst, most persistent hurt was emotional and psychological. It became my mission in life to kill this pain by any means possible.

I started growing pot in a well-hidden location about 200 metres (650 feet) upstream from my camp. The benefits were twofold: drugging myself was a way of self-medicating against the agony of a shattered life, and the cash crop gave me the means to purchase a few comforts, including booze. By then I'd started having limited contact with people I called "the fringe dwellers" – the smattering of hippies and outsiders who lived in and around the "alternative lifestyle" communities dotted along the north coast of New South Wales.

Every few months or so, I'd venture into the towns to trade with them, swapping marijuana for food and alcohol, or both. Sometimes I'd offload enough pot to bankroll a bigger purchase, like my DIY bush brewery. I'd been a raging alcoholic for at least a decade by this time, but trying to wash away my troubles with alcohol cost money that I didn't always have. Ever focused on "killing the pain", I needed to find a cheap solution to staying drunk in the forest.

One day I lit on the idea of brewing my own beer, like my alcoholic father had done when I was a boy. I purchased a plastic garbage bin, a sheet, a thermometer, sugar and a home-brew starter kit, and dragged it all back up to the mountain. Using water from the creek (some of it boiled in a tin over the fire), I half-filled the garbage bin at the correct temperature, added the sugar and home brew, stirred it with a stick and covered it with the sheet. Three or four days later, I had about 30 litres (53 pints) of "beer". It tasted foul and induced a gag reflex, but I managed to keep it down and it had the desired effect. I had turned my creek into a river of alcohol.

While I deemed drink and drugs essential to the management of emotional trauma, I had to keep myself in check. Falling off the cliff was a real danger, but aside from that, hermit life requires a fair amount of planning and constant effort.

There was no one to do the chores for me. I had to gather firewood pretty much every day and cut fresh ferns for my bed whenever the mattress began to rot. I had to gather, prepare and store my food, tend to the brewery and manage the marijuana crop during the summer months. The fire needed plenty of love, too, but above all I had to work hard at avoiding detection.

I developed animal-like instincts when it came to covering my tracks. As well as regulating my smoke output and foraging further afield, I never made a trail of any kind in or around my secret gully. Wherever possible I would traverse the terrain by hopping from rock to rock or log to log, and I never took a step that would leave a footprint. As my connection to the forest strengthened, I became so tuned in to the ecosystem that I could roam through the bush at night without fear of breaking a spider's web, let alone a twig or a branch.

Other senses sharpened, too. My hearing became highly sensitive to nature's finer frequencies. I could detect changes in wind direction by the sound it made in the leaves around me. I could differentiate between the soft sounds snakes and lizards made in the undergrowth, and I came to learn the full songbook of countless native birds. I began most days listening to their recitals and I noticed the playlist changed in accordance with the seasons and migrations. The power of such a musical shift could affect my mood or change the way I approached my day.

There was one sound, however – an eerie, high-pitched squeal – that took me much longer to identify, and it used to scare the hell out of me. I'd hear it in all corners of the forest but more so at night, particularly if there was a breeze. At dawn, I'd set off in the direction of the previous night's blood-curdling shriek in the hope of finding a trace of the creature that had made it. I always came back empty-handed. Ultimately, I decided it had to be aliens.

One day, as I walked along an old logging trail on the eastern side of the mountain, I heard the noise louder than ever before. It chilled me to the bone because it was so close, overhead and just a little way off the track. I swallowed my fear and quietly pushed through the undergrowth. I braced for an encounter with an alien when the terrible squeal split the air again. My eyes shot in the direction of the din, right above my head. The "extraterrestrial" turned out to be nothing more than the branches of neighbouring gum trees rubbing against each other in the wind. The long-term mystery was solved. It was the first time I'd laughed out loud in years.

I developed something of a marsupial nose, too. At its core, the forest was an endless cycle of death and renewal, and each living plant and animal had its own scent as it moved through the various stages of existence. A sapling, for example, smelled different to a mature, dying or dead tree of the same species. Even water gave off a different aroma depending on its state in the forest. A stagnant waterhole, a running creek, mist in the gully and raindrops on leaves each smelled totally different to me. There was one odour, however, that set alarm bells clanging in my head – that of humans. I'd detect the smell of their cigarettes long before their clumsy footfalls crashed into my domain. Naturally I'd be long gone before they ever got close.

For all the spirituality, the oneness with nature, the glorious autonomy and the rewiring of my nervous system, I was still a homeless man. I was still an alcoholic. I was still an addict and still estranged from everything and everyone in the world. After eight or nine years of forest life, I started to come apart at the seams like an old battered raincoat. That's when the aliens decided it was time to intervene.

————————

There is only so much punishment the human mind and body can take, and I had treated mine so egregiously for so long that the demise was frighteningly dramatic. Malnutrition had reduced me to skin and bones. A near complete lack of protein, combined with a constant and crippling gastric problem from drinking creek-water moonshine, had left me weak, fatigued and stooped. I needed a stick to stand upright. Almost all of my teeth had rotted away in my jaws. Over the years I'd literally plucked the loose ones out and thrown them away. They're still up on the mountain today playing their small role in the ageless cycle of death and renewal. As time wore on, I figured it wouldn't be long before I, too, decayed and turned to dust on the forest floor.

I began to fray mentally as well as physically. A lifetime of trauma and self-abuse had finally caught up with me. Depression, post-traumatic stress, chronic anxiety, social dislocation, exhaustion, near starvation and the barrage of mind-altering drugs and alcohol I had thrown at my problems had led me down a long and twisted road to psychosis.

I was mindlessly fidgeting with some twigs and pebbles at the fireside one day when my ancestors first appeared at the camp. They were humanoid and as real to my eyes and ears as any person I'd ever met. We didn't need introductions because I knew who they were: they were me. They were me from 100 years ago, 1,000 years ago. They were me from the beginning of time, and they radiated pure love.

Some were Druids and some of the ancient ones wore adornments of bronze, lead and copper in their hair. There were four main beings that day. During later visits there were sometimes fewer and sometimes more, but whenever they came by, we'd talk for hours. No topic was off limits, and they were patient as

I ranted and complained about the unfairness of life. Over the course of a year, the conversation narrowed to one main topic: my estrangement from the world and the ancestors' desire for me to return to it.

One night, as I sat next to the fire, they came straight to the point: "If you stay up here you could die." I resisted the encouragement to save myself, of course – just like I did when the aliens had raised the topic. They'd also started turning up unannounced in 1998–9. Pale, thin, genderless creatures, they'd glide silently through the bush and somehow avoid getting dirty. I was less tolerant of the aliens, mostly because they were pushier and more persistent than the ancestors. Every time I'd come up with a reason to stay in the forest and die, they'd dismantle my arguments with calm reason and crystal-clear logic.

I may have preferred the company of the ancestors, but in the end it was the aliens who convinced me to leave. They agreed with my argument that death in itself wasn't a problem. The real concern, they said, was held in the hearts of others. There were people who loved me – I had a daughter and four sisters somewhere. If I lay down and died where I was, they would never know what happened to me. Such a hurt, they said, would never go away.

I couldn't argue with that.

It might have been days later, or weeks or months, but I eventually staggered back into society. I have no recollection of the exact moment, or if I even said goodbye to the forest – only that I woke up in a hospital bed completely broken, emaciated, scared and close to death … but still, somehow, with the chance to start over.

It's getting on for a quarter of a century since I came down from the mountain. Finding my way through the jungle of modern cities has been a challenge but one I commit to every day. At first I tried and failed to get a job. It wasn't just the wild look of my long hair and beard. Time and time again my lack of experience and education tripped me up. I realized if I wanted to progress in life I needed to be educated – quite a tall order for a homeless man of 45.

Slowly I set about the task. I quit drugs and alcohol for good and gradually regained the weight and mental stability I'd lost in the forest. By putting one foot in front of the other I managed, over 15 years, to gain a university degree and then a doctorate in sociology. Along the way I cautiously opened my heart and let other human beings in – for the first time in my life. I found mentors among the academics, friendships with other students, and family, by reuniting with my daughter and my long-lost little sisters.

Although the forest is in my past, the years I spent there continue to inform my decisions and the man I choose to be today. Living alone in the wilderness brought the human condition into sharp focus for me. Trust me, once you've survived in the wild over a long period, you'll never take society for granted again.

Being something of a hunter-gatherer for all those years taught me the true value of food, and just how hard it can be to come by in nature. I expended enormous amounts of physical and mental energy killing in order to survive for another day. I still get blown away by the ease of consumption on offer at the local supermarket. Sometimes I think if a giant switch was thrown and humanity was suddenly forced to fend for itself the way I had, millions upon millions would starve to death.

Although I briefly ate meat to put on weight in the early days of my recovery, I have largely kept my vow to the animal kingdom. Today, aged 67, I'm a sober, chemical-free vegetarian – and far healthier than I've been for a long time because I understand what my body needs in terms of nutrition.

I am spiritually fitter, too. As much as I regret it, I can't bring back all the creatures I destroyed to eat but I do think about them a lot, and I sometimes quietly thank them for sustaining me during my darkest days. Where I was once a violent and threatening person, I walk far more gently in the world nowadays. This is partly due to my study of, and interest in, sociology (I chose the subject at university to try to understand why society and I hated each other so much!). But my gentler approach was also born of my time in the forest where I dared not disturb my surroundings or leave a trace of my passage.

I conduct my life now with a similar outlook. I clean up after myself in the physical sense and I try never to leave a mess in a person's heart or mind, either. In the forest I eschewed making a footprint and it's the same out here in the real world. I prefer a small life when it comes to the planet's natural resources. I have a place off-grid on a plot of regrowth forest not too far from the university where I teach. My two-room shack runs on solar and battery power. I harvest rainwater from the sky, eggs from my chickens and fruit from my small orchard.

When it comes to my heart, however, I revel in a much larger existence. I've connected with a beautiful new family and I feel enormously privileged to be on my life's journey with them.

I'm still woken by the birds most days and I'm as much in love with their greatest hits as I ever was. The sound of nature is everywhere, if you can learn to turn down all the other noise. I'm getting a little older and my hearing isn't as sharp as it was during my hermit years, but I instinctively tune in and meditate to the sound of wind, rain, thunder and the silence of open spaces. It reminds me I'm a tiny part of a grand natural cycle, a strand of DNA in a spiral that spans all of time.

My spirituality remains bound to the ancestors and aliens who came to me in the forest – whether they appeared due to psychosis or not. Had they not implored me to give society another chance, I'd have died in the ferns and dirt 23 years ago. How could I not rejoice at such loving interventions? I've been back to the forest a few times over the years but the ancient elders were long gone, even though the stones of the fireplace were still there. It's a good thing, then, that I carry them in my heart.

I've learned a huge amount from my intense relationship with Mother Nature – admittedly much of it about what not to do. In her grace she opened my eyes to immense beauty and exposed me to sheer terror. She gifted me serenity and freedom but slapped me hard when I took her for granted. Hell, she kept me alive for ten ridiculous years! Her greatest gift, however, was showing me that no matter how much we may fight it, we are not meant to face life alone.

SOULCRAFT

Nature — the other nature we call "the wild" — has always been the essential element and the primary setting of the journey to soul. The soul, after all, is our inner wilderness, the intrapsychic terrain we know the least that holds our individual mysteries. When we truly enter the outer wild — fully opened to its enigmatic and feral powers — the soul responds with its own cries and cravings. These passions might frighten us at first because they threaten to upset the carefully assembled applecart of our conventional lives. Perhaps this is why many people regard their souls in much the same way they view deserts, jungles, oceans, wild mountains and dark forests — as dangerous and forbidding places.

Our society is forever erecting barriers between its citizens and the inner/outer wilderness. On the outer side we have our air-conditioned houses and automobiles, gated communities and indoor malls, fences and animal control officers, dams and virtual realities. On the inner side we're offered prescribed "mood enhancers", alcohol and street drugs; consumerism and dozens of other soul-numbing addictions; fundamentalisms, transcendentalisms and other escapisms; rigid belief systems as to what is "good" and what is "bad"; and teachings that God or some other paternal figure will watch over us and protect our delicate lives.

But when we escape beyond these artificial barriers, we discover something astonishing: nature and soul not only depend on each other but long for each other and are, in the end, the same substance, like twins or trees sharing the same roots. The individual soul is the core of our human nature, the reason for which we were born, the essence of our specific life purpose, and ours alone. Yet our true nature is first a mystery to our everyday mind. To recover our inmost secrets, we must venture into the inner/outer wilderness, where we shall find our essential nature waiting for us.

From *Soulcraft* by Bill Plotkin. 2003
© Bill Plotkin.

Reprinted with permission of
New World Library, Novato, CA.
www.newworldlibrary.com

Bill Plotkin is a depth psychologist and wilderness guide from the US. He is the founder of Colorado's Animas Valley Institute, taking people on journeys into the mysteries of nature and the psyche.

Jennifer has been a professional classical soloist since 2009, performing internationally. After moving to Berlin to pursue a career in opera, she experienced a traumatic event that changed her life. She is now pursuing a new path in healing through music and nature connection at her home in Tuscany.

This is a story which shows how the mythical non-human world is helping her to heal after her trauma.

LOST AND FOUND
JENNIFER JOOSTEN-BRISK

I am sitting in this place, familiar yet new, and I wonder, how did I get here? An ancient stone farmhouse, a medieval village and miles and miles of countryside. The house is a little ramshackle in parts; walls lean askew, half a metre (1½ feet) thick in some rooms. There are secret passages, strange doors with huge iron keys and interesting markings on the walls. Some of the windows leak and look like they've shrunk away from their frames, almost sad, with their shutters drooping. Outside is a garden, a jumble of colours and textures and sounds. Full of enchantments and surprises.

"I've never seen anything like this in my life," I mumble to myself, still wondering how I got here. My husband and I have just left a huge part of our lives behind us in the big, bold city of Berlin. While we make this transition, he will commute from there and then on to Amsterdam for work. So I'm here alone to get started on the house. But where do I start? What have I got us into here?

Feeling overwhelmed by the endless colours, the endless to-do list, boilers that won't start, gas that seems to be leaking from goodness-knows-where, electricity that keeps blowing or worryingly sparking from plugs and sockets, I aim for the garden to escape it all. I look around and breathe deeply into my dusty, city lungs, yet I am far from the Altbau apartment on Paul-Lincke-Ufer in Berlin, where I would lean over the balcony to catch glimpses of ducks on the Maybachufer canal, and of crowds passing busily beneath. This was so still and quiet. Another world almost. I see bright white rays of sun darting onto a nearby flowering apricot tree, the white of its petals glowing incandescent in the sunshine. The garden seems magical and so much like the gardens I had seen before in childhood stories. I feel as though I could be a character in one of those stories now, walking around secret gardens, talking to the animals in mysterious worlds. It invites me to forget myself and my worries and takes me away from time, as though I'm a carefree child again. I feel connected to who I really am here, away from the city's enticements.

I climb up and balance on a nearby crumbling wall and see how the garden unfolds toward the greater landscape, with its valleys and hills and forests that lie thick and dark along them. The mountains beyond wear dark woods like a cloak, hiding within them wild beasts, flora, fauna, streams and waterfalls. The forests are filled with mystery and magic. And it calls to me. I feel this pull, a tug inside me, to stir me off the periphery where I stand and move toward it. Toward what I am in awe of, maybe also afraid of, of nature, of everything that I feel now I am here. I want to connect to it, to something bigger than me, also part of me.

The church bells ring and a quarrel of sparrows are startled from a hedge. They tumble and dart out in feathery bundles from the leafy laurel into the road. They dive upward above the olive grove treetops and behind the church. I feel as though with their excited energy they are summoning me to follow them out of the garden and into action with them. "Come with us," I feel them twittering to me. The promise of excitement lures me out and I look toward the birds and the cloaked hills beyond. Nature draws me out of myself. The pathways and the tracks that lead out toward the hills stretch further still onto the mighty snow-covered slopes of the Apennine mountains. Delicious gusts of cool, wet spring air thrill my nostrils as they swirl down from the icy caps beyond. As if with little tendrils and hooks the air is capturing me, pulling me along. It feels as though I am being carted off by a gang of invisible fairies or mythical creatures I can't see. I just let them guide me.

As I walk I can smell lavender, stirring from its winter hibernation, a note of thyme and sage, a whiff of rosemary and warming rose bushes, and fragrant flowers with tiny buds are starting to appear. I observe the empty vines with tiny cone-shaped buds emerging, all crooked and barren after wintertime, leaning on terraces adjacent to the evergreen olive groves beneath the road. I descend through the ancient terraces of yet more ancient trees and moss-covered, century-old dry-stone walls. My white-grey rubber boots are meeting with dirt, stone, moss, leaves, grass … The still-cold air of last season is blowing into the early spring landscape and it refreshes my spirit. It enlivens me and wipes away the stress of my old daily life. Glued to bright screens scrolling through endless emails, messages, making calls, long to-do lists, deadlines, pressures … This is stepping into another world, going through the wardrobe with Lucy from the Narnia chronicles. I am taking her hand and going with her, feeling the fear, the excitement, pushing aside the heavy fur coats, leaving behind my family and friends and the noisy world of my previous life, and walking through to the back of that wardrobe into this, into Narnia, where I always dreamed to be.

As I'm thinking about Lucy, a little robin flies onto a nearby branch of an olive tree hanging over the path ahead of me, and chirps cheerily. I feel like she is guiding me on, and she is part of that network of mythical beings taking me along this walk, away from my new house in these strange and fascinating Italian hills and into the adventure I've been waiting for. The sun is getting warmer and I feel my body heating up beneath the layers I am wearing. I look down at my feet as they cross a small downhill stream that flows over the path I am taking. I let my boots sit on the rounded stones and feel the cold of the water slowly transfer through the neoprene onto my skin. It helps cool me down a little and reminds me of childhood moments of joy. Jumping into puddles in boots.

I hear a light chirping and see my robin again, bouncing on a slim drooping branch of olive and cheering me on once again. I smile at her and carry on walking, heading further down the hill toward the woods of pine trees, chestnuts and oaks. I start to increase the speed of my stride as I gain in confidence and feel like I'm really on the right route. I'm heading toward the little medieval village below, then I can go back up another hill in a loop through the woods that should bring me back home. I feel as though I've tapped into some inner navigation system that is pulling me along.

By the time I get to the village, I'm surprised to see that everything is closed and there's no one about, nowhere to buy water or food as I had hoped when I set off. I didn't bring enough water with me. I had no idea I'd been walking for 2 hours already. As I'm now heading uphill, the cool breeze of the mountains is still beyond me. I'm thirsty under the hot sun; it's so bright it hurts my eyes. I strain to read signs of where I am to go next. I look around the quiet village but the fountain that most villages have states that the water is *non potabile*; luckily I know that means "not drinkable". A moment of panic strikes. "Oh my god," I burst out. I hope I'm not doing it again, getting myself into life-and-death situations. How do I always manage to do this? What on earth is wrong with me? I actually have no definite idea of how to get back. I feel my confidence draining. I probably should have been sensible and brought a map at least, and more water. Okay, I can always just walk back the way I came. I can be sensible, that is an option. After all, this is an Italian village in Tuscany, not a desert.

After calming myself down on a nearby bench in the shade, and consulting Pocket Earth for some proper navigation, I feel I have an idea of how far it is to return through the higher forest paths. I roughly calculate that I can make it before dark if I speed up, and now manage to convince myself everything is fine and I can do this. I can walk through a forest and get back to my empty farmhouse on the hill, on the other side of this valley. (The days of cycling around Berlin's mostly flat, busy streets seem like a distant memory.) The trail ahead isn't too steep or too high, it seems. Our house sits at around 400 metres (1,300 feet) above sea level and this pass apparently goes up to around 500 metres (1,640 feet), a mere hill. I was heading toward Monte Albereta (540 metres/1,770 feet) but now plan to cut through the forest down onto a path that should get me back to my village. Then hopefully on to a big, steaming teapot full of Yorkshire Gold tea, with digestive biscuits, in front of my warm, crackling fire. Fit for the storytelling that would ensue.

Still in the gentle trail of hills, I think of the grand Apuan Alps nearby and the higher Apennine mountain peaks, where my husband decided to propose to me. I'd nearly collapsed in terror on the way up, thinking I'd have a heart attack. I was so grateful to be alive, of course, that I said yes! I also think back to being on Mount Meru (4,660 metres/1,528 feet) where he took me in Africa on a tour of the places he used to live as a child. It was truly one of the scariest things I'd done but also one of the most magnificent; watching the sun come up over Kilimanjaro changes you. My stoic Dutch husband is the real adventurer here. Despite knowing about my terror of heights, and of just about anything wild and unfamiliar, he nonetheless has taken me on some real-world adventures. I guess moving our lives here was my turn to conduct a big adventure. Sometimes we know it's time to confront our fears, stretch our comfort zone, and step into the unknown; this was my unknown.

As I leave the small sleeping village behind me on the forest trail, I feel once again connected to that tugging feeling. The trail is leading me through a beautiful, seemingly empty forest. I meet with a silence but one full of strange music. It is peaceful music and I forget about my anxieties. Little woodland springs burst through the ground and trickle down toward narrow brooks, pouring over stones and soil and leaves. There are scatterings of ferns in amber and green, little naked bushes with bright red berries, and thick swathes of undergrowth, caught up in vines and thorny tangles. With each breath I feel I'm inhaling medicine, each breath so clean and fresh. The forest has a scent that seems so familiar, so calming that I feel my body easing and my mind clearing, emptying. Although I still feel hot inside my clothes and sweat profusely, I realize I am in awe, observing the cycle of early spring. Nature is bursting back into life all around me. The woods are full of a magnetic energy and a rich history that I am just passing through, merging with, and sucking up. I feel reborn. I'm tapping into something lost in me, something primal, something forgotten; it is awakening. As I cross over more gurgling streams, beneath canopies of gnarled old oaks, chestnuts and pines in this ancient and dense woodland, I imagine the Etruscans who would have hunted here for the famous wild boars. As I step through the hunters' tracks, I see the hundreds of little hoof prints of the boars sunk into the mud. I feel closer and closer to their wild world, to ancient traditions, and I am now at the place where it all meets.

I think this could be where medieval knights would have fought neighbouring foes to defend their territories, and I imagine how life evolved further away from these places, further away from nature and into cities and technologies. How has this changed us, I wonder? I realize I'm humming to myself happily and almost skipping along the track. Then I hear something. Suddenly, a darkness grabs at my heart and shakes the peace within it. I stop still and stop smiling. I long for the little robin to fly back onto my path and cheer me along again, to be closer to home. But I'm alone and maybe even lost, and time is passing so quickly the air is already cooling down a little. My perspiration is giving me a little chill. I look quickly around and don't know what to expect. A thousand news reports flash through my mind about women alone in woods, and they grip me in their terror. Is there someone else here? What can I do? I have no signal and my Pocket Earth is running on GPS. I am really alone here. I panic and start walking fast and hope it was just a rabbit. I'm already in the grips of fear when I hear it again. I spin my head around toward the direction the noise is coming from. I can barely hear over the sudden pounding thuds of my heart. Then I see it.

I see a deer staring at me, frozen still, from the thickets above my trail and on a mildly slanting incline. It must have darted into a thorny net of bushes and become caught up in the tangled vines growing downward from the tree above. We stare at each other, both terrified, both suspended in that moment. It is a roe deer, I notice, small and more discreet than the heavier-footed fallow deer that I can hear in the fields around our house at night. Her gentle brown fur is pulled tightly across her taut body. She has long, spindly legs and her big black eyes look like large pools suspended in her small skull. The dark pools are shiny and flash as she pulls her skull tightly upward in an abrupt tilt, looking upward for an escape. She is a delicate being. I'm concerned she might hurt herself on the thorns if I scare her further, and I don't know how to react so I just stare, my mind racing. It is an incredible moment. I can see her quick breath swelling and contracting her rib cage, and the faint outline of her bones emerging through fine pelt. She begins to struggle. I see fear in her eyes and wish to console her. "I won't hurt you," I murmur. I feel my own fear assuage as I reflect on her helplessness. It occurs to me that in different circumstances she would be very right to fear me. I am, in fact, a predator. The thought startles me, and I feel guilt as I confront the truth that I did eat meat. I feel sorry for that. I assure her again , "I won't hurt you." Her presence restores my humanity.

She eventually yanks herself free. She springs off with a great muscular leap, up and beyond the dense brush and foliage, darting off in angular motions, dodging other thorny nets and knotted shrubs. She is gone. My eyes follow her as best they can in the hope of catching a last glimpse, to check if she was hurt or is happily free. I want her to be free. A moment later I notice an old wooden sign, grown over and faded, chipped and rather weathered. It points to an overgrown path I wasn't intending to take. I look at my phone and realize that this path will lead me on a shortcut back to my village, if it isn't blocked further on by fallen trees and impassable thickets. "Thank you, deer," I whisper gratefully to her, and begin my careful descent home.

Before I manage even a few hundred metres, I feel drops of moisture land on me through the netted canopy of branches and leaves above. Abruptly, it pours down from seemingly nowhere onto my head. It feels as though a shower or a hose has just been aimed right at me. "Oh my god, what's happening?" I say out loud. I need to get back fast. It's getting dark now and I'm still feeling a little nervous and dazed from my encounter. How can it just rain like that so suddenly and so heavily, through so many layers of trees? I'm getting soaked and feel stupid running down this abandoned path. I'm grateful that no one is around to see how ridiculous I look. I'm praying I can get back before the dark sets in. I realize as I jog along in my rubber boots that I'm actually feeling elated; elated at being soaked in the rain, elated by the smell of the wet earth as it fills my nostrils with moist air, elated by the joy of being alone and free, and elated at seeing this beautiful beast, staring at me and somehow connected to me.

I cherish the sacred moment of acknowledgement in which the roe deer had really looked into my eyes and somehow guided me home. I wonder, could it be? I look again at my boots, covered in dirt and magically keeping me upright despite the sodden earth beneath them and the wet, slippery stones jutting through it. I begin to laugh. I'm not sure why but in the heavy downpour I see myself, covered in dirt, sweat-soaked, rain-soaked, scared, maybe lost, and it suddenly comes back to me, a memory of who I was. I'm back there, in my old life. Still laughing in the woods at the same time. I'm back on the concert platform. With a shiny satin red dress, red lips made up and sparkling earrings. I'm walking onto the stage, the audience applauding, and I take my well-rehearsed bow. I'm wearing my dark-red velvet-lined heels, fitting snugly around warm, swollen feet; this is the finale of a great concert. I breathe deeply but quietly as I am bowed, so the audience does not see or hear, then I slowly release my breath as I rise back into a standing position. I align my shoulders subtly, I release my lower back, tilt the pelvis slightly backward as I let the air fill my lower abdomen, my diaphragm straightens, and I hold it as I release my jaw. The piano begins, the pianist knows me and knows when to start, we breathe together until my first note sails out of my throat and fills the auditorium. I'm back there in that memory as my boots carry me home, through the healing wilds of nature. But I allow the thought, I allow myself to feel the fear of being the performer again – that moment before you arrive onto the stage where you are constricted, then that moment as you walk out. I feel it in my fear of being here now alone. I let it merge together, the past and the present. I tell myself how funny it all is, and being here makes so much more sense to me now.

The opera singer, scurrying around soaked and tired and scared, getting lost in the middle of nowhere. No real map. A wet iPhone. Miles and miles with no water or food. No knowledge of the area. What was I thinking, doing this? I go back again to the red dress; I remember the feel of the satin on my skin, the perspiration above my lip, the beads that drip down my temples beneath my hair, as they do now. I'm fully alert and fully alive as I bellow out my highest notes and hear my voice travelling around the concert hall and back to me. I blend the audience's faces into one mass and slightly blur my eyes to avoid direct contact with individual glances. I have to stay in the flow, in the deep connection to my breath, to my body, and the battle is to stay in that space and not let fear overtake. I realize in that moment that these states of focus tie together the two worlds; they are not as far apart as they seem. The singing connects you to your body and your breath, it grounds you as being out in nature does. The state of flow in which you are deeply focused on detail, and yet connected below and above to outer energies, is the same connection here in the forest. Being alert, concentrated, connected to breath and in another state of mind in which flow can take over, daily minutiae obscured and you find yourself in equanimity, collected, calm, composed. Almost solid, like the trees, my body flexible but unbreakable and my roots growing downward as my voice soared upward, as my spirit soars now being here, my voice soared out into the music hall there. In those moments I'm like the natural world around me, whole. Walking onto the stage I'm like the deer, both afraid and caught, but then, when I dig in and connect, I rise above fear and feel stillness and strength. That's what I have here too; there is the bridge between these worlds.

I must rise above fear now as it is already darkening. The rain isn't easing as I had hoped but becoming more of a monsoon as time passes. "You have courage, Jen," I tell myself. I hear the pianist's last notes, I bow again, I look at the swollen veins in my feet and the skin gathering at the edges of the now tight shoes, I feel the perspiration run onto my face and I slowly stand and walk away, triumphant. The audience applauds loudly. I wait backstage and listen to the cheers and feel elated. I tell myself, "Jen, if you could do that, then of course you can do this!" You are calling upon those same resources.

Finally I can see in the now dark-grey sky and powdery rain that there are lights appearing. They seem high up as I am descending the wet woodland trail. I hear the chatter of various birds and wonder where they are hiding in this deluge. Seeing the lights fills me with a sense of deep relief; I realize they are the lights of the Santa Zita Oratorio. It is a little, yellow, oval-shaped church said to be the birthplace of a famous Lucan saint, Santa Zita. She is represented by the little flowers that look like daisies here, the little *ziti* I think they call them in the village. They are popping through the grass now at this time of year. I feel the lights of the church are guiding me safely back and I'm so grateful to her and her presence here, especially now. A good, kind spirit. The simple way of life she symbolized, of being connected directly to nature, connects the people here to themselves too, I realize. I love that they celebrate here every year, celebrate her life and nature. They burn huge bonfires and dance and sing and attend Mass. It's wonderful to be part of these sacred rituals around nature. A celebration of symbiosis. I feel more connected to myself and to nature by just being here and observing it all. The people live from the land now as they did then, honouring their ancient customs and traditions. They have a deep respect for their land and a synergy with it. I admire their knowledge and skills at living from the earth in this way and admire how they have continued those traditions for their children and their grandchildren. A precious legacy. They grow fruits and vegetables, and care for the horses and donkeys, the goats that give milk and the chickens that provide eggs. I hope to learn so much from them. I can now smell the animals and the damp straw and manure in the air, as I wind my way slowly down the path and begin to recognize my neighbours' houses. I can almost see the white smoke mixing into the darkened sky. I can smell it filling the air with its soot and resins and I'm quietly comforted. I enjoy this feeling of being soaked through to the bone, and although I'm now cold I enjoy that feeling too – so alien to me from the instant comforts and luxuries I was accustomed to in the city lifestyle that I walked away from.

As I approach the little village road with its potholes and cracks and running drains that seem to be flooded, I laugh to myself again. This is my life now. No more buzzing, throbbing cities, full of people and things. No more frantic schedule. I'm skipping down a road in soaking wet clothes like a child, shaking with the cold, and I've left that other life behind me. I spent nearly all my life, until this point, building that old dream, lost in that pursuit of a life I'm not sure I ever really wanted. But leaving it all and coming here was still such a risk. So many people didn't understand why I would leave all that behind – the career I'd wanted for so long that I was finally getting there with. I think of the effort it took to build that up, to get to that level, and also of my husband's career. But had I really ever wanted it? Had he? Growing up, I'd just wanted to run away into the hills beyond all the towns and villages to freedom, to nature. I wanted to run away from school, from normality; I always felt trapped by it and always felt lost. But how do you explain that, if you don't really know what you mean and everyone else is going with the flow. How do you know you're lost if there doesn't seem to be another way?

I realize I'm now on the little road that runs alongside my back garden and nearly home; it's such a relief. The smoke from the chimneys is stronger now and there's another peculiar smell of burning. There's a very present, pungent stench of smoke that reminds me of the pollution of the city. As I look around, my mind switches back again and I think of the city we left and the real reasons why we did it.

Suddenly I look down at my feet to catch my balance as I trip into a crack in the road. In a flash the boots are gone, my feet now bare and blood-stained. I try to stabilize myself. A metallic odour fills my nose as I inhale in panicked, short breaths. "Help!" I scream for what seems like an eternity, trapped by terror and circumstance. I'm trembling now, not with the cold but with shock as I watch my beautiful husband collapse to the ground and close his eyes. It's an image that fills me with dread; my heart bangs loudly against my ribcage and adrenaline pumps through my veins. My mind is again aflood with memories. I remember that fateful accident that changed everything and ended that old life for me. It now becomes obvious how it is connected to me being here now. My heart feels suddenly heavy again and I feel tears flooding through my eyes onto my wet face. I think of the accident again. Life can change in a fraction of a second. The heavy rain is now a constant drizzle, and my clothes feel heavy on my shoulders and on my skin. I replay again how my husband fell off the ladder; I play it on repeat like a clip of a movie. I watch again as he falls through the glass door in our new home, the home we'd planned to start a family in, to live out our lives. We'd been renovating it for over a year and we were so happy it was finished, so eager to move in. After years of searching I felt I'd carved out a perfect life; I'd found a passion and I'd found love. Our apartment was our nest and I'd been gathering all the twigs and leaves and putting it all together for us. But on the very first morning of our new life, my husband was battling for his life. It felt like a nightmare. He had fallen from the ladder and through a glass panel in our bedroom door while rushing to let the builders in. He hadn't put on his glasses and was still sleepy. He had lost his balance. I'll never forget the horror of those moments, confronted by the life and death of someone you deeply love and being suddenly responsible for their survival while frozen in panic.

I feel my body heave and sigh and sob as I remember his screams and then my scream for help. It felt like an eternity. My boots keep me moving homeward and stop me from just falling to the ground in sobs. But it wasn't a straightforward journey from there to here. I try to make all the dots connect but they won't; life isn't like that – it doesn't play out in straight lines how we expect it to. It's still not absolutely straightforward and it's all been full of doubt and self-conflict. I remember the shock later of losing my voice. Of the surgeon tapping me gently on the knee after examining my vocal cords. I can still see pictures of him with Joan Sutherland and shaking hands with Pavarotti, hanging on the wall behind him. And there he was, in his office, tapping me on the knee with a knowing smile and me still full of hope, when he said, "I'm afraid it's not good news." I feel the dread even now. It can't be true. I hadn't read that in his face. It can't be; he's joking. I have flights booked and paid for to go to Hong Kong. I have a lead role to perform and I have concerts in Italy. "You have exploded blood vessels all over your vocal cords, and you have nodules on both sides, scarring and blisters. You can't go," he said to me in a clear and directive voice. "You will have to have surgery immediately and stop singing." I felt sick inside.

The journey from that night onward, as I cycled past forests on my way home in the dark, took me through fear, anxiety, hopelessness, identity crisis-ness, depression and despair, because a giant pillar holding up my sense of safety and my sense of self was pulled out from underneath me. Without singing, who was I? Nobody. Without my husband would I even want to live? Was it all my fault? Could I have helped more? All because of a ladder, such a trivial, seemingly inconsequential object. Nearly losing him and then losing my voice, I was abruptly confronted with the fragility and changeability of life. I wanted to go away from the city, the performing, the stages, the applause, the striving and competing, and all the constant pressure and stress that come from upholding other people's expectations and striving for validation. Was it possible just to walk away from that and from everything? And then I saw it with clarity – well, why not? Who's going to stop me? Why can't I just leave the city, leave my job and go and find Narnia, find nature, to make my deepest and real dreams come true. Put fear aside.

Then it was obvious – we were to go to Italy. Do something crazy, like find a farmhouse. Idyllic scenes from movies swirled in our minds as we made plans, got advice, and got excited about the idea of finally growing vegetables and getting a dog and chickens, maybe even starting a family. We stirred up all the usual fantasies of picturesque country life that we had talked of in the past. But this time we were really going to do it, we had to seize this moment.

I find myself at home already, getting logs from my wood store in the now dark garden. I'm trembling but still pleased to be alone, up in the Tuscan hills, hidden away in an old farmhouse, and by a sacred site. I feel so, so far away from the world of opera and of cities, of the busy doing, doing, doing. I feel I can be my real self here. I don't have to perform anymore; I don't have to try to be a level of perfection I can't attain. I can just exist and feel stillness and acceptance in myself. I get flashes of being screamed at by a director, memories of conductors yelling at me, being humiliated by teachers, of missing entrances and being terrified, of feeling intimidated by orchestras and choirs, and the terror of walking out onto that platform alone. I think of myself as a child wanting Narnia and magic and escape into nature, and see I took a wrong turn. I think of school and how I hated it, and felt so pressured to achieve and to be somebody, to prove my worth. My schooling didn't really cater for someone highly sensitive or creative; it didn't include subjects that would help me really understand our place in nature and the universe beyond. Here I'm now foraging in the dark, grappling with wet piles of logs, hoping nothing springs out from beneath them, like snakes have recently, or big spiders or rain-soaked scorpions. I see I've made it through the gauntlet of the day and this garden is my Narnia. No matter where my journey has taken me so far, this is where I've landed and it is healing. Nature helps you repair all your broken bits.

I hear the kettle whistling from inside the house. I barely remember filling it. I stand up with my basket full of damp logs. It quickly sounds more like a screech that rings loudly out into the garden as I rush back to the house. I savour the moment of propping my feet up in front of the blazing fire and sip my tea as my eyes slowly attune to its warm flickers. As it glows out of the dark fireplace, I go back to the forest and look again for my deer. I see her there once more. Her huge, dark eyes stare into me as I stare now into the flames. I look down at my own angular limbs and form and see my chest swell with each breath. I realize how similar we are. Her tawny pelt covering her elegant bones, concealing the same flesh and blood beneath as mine. Her delicate skull lifted, searching for danger with those bewildered eyes, the thudding heart, locked in her fear. I think about how my own fear has locked me into my life in the past. But she escaped, she was able to free herself from those tangled snares, to bolt off with her lithe muscular hind legs and sprint away from threat. How alike we really are. Both survivors. Looking for sanctuary in nature, alert and careful. Her mind was connected to that same ancient wisdom: instinct. Whispers and echoes of which are enmeshed in our DNA. It had protected her and led her to safety, as it had for me.

NATURE WHISPER TO MY EARS

GABRIELLA GARCIA

Let go child, said the wind.
Shuuuuuaaaaaa, shuuuuuaaaa.
Travel with me between worlds,
The physical and the spiritual worlds.

You are creating vibrations.
Every moment,
Every sound,
That comes out,
from your throat.

Follow the moon cycle,
Said the ocean.
Observe the tides.
You'll know when to go inwards.
And when is time to be out again.

Remember the Eclipse is a time to be still.
The Full Moon is a time to celebrate.
And the New Moon is a time to plant.

Go back to the magic forest,
Said the mushroom,
As often as possible.

I find myself sitting on the grass…

Remember to release,
What doesn't serve you,
Back to the Earth.
She will absorb it.
And transform it.

You are the breath,
Within the breath.
My Child.
Burn your fears,
On the wildfire.
Let it run Wild.

Stand tall, said the mountain.
Let the sunshine open your crown,
And the light travel through your body.

In the dark, I saw many guardians.
Watching the night.

See yourself on every leaf.
On every face.
On every flower.
Feel the unity.
The oneness within all.

Nature Whisper to My Ears © Gabriella Garcia, 2023

**Gabriella is a project manager from Nicaragua with
a passion for writing. Having trained as a medical
professional, she unplugged from the matrix in 2018, to
explore belonging and the creation of a new culture.**

Rupert lives in the southwest of the UK and has had a lifelong love of reweaving threads of connection with the more-than-human world. His background is in environmental and outdoor education with an emphasis on eco-psychological approaches to exploring ecological identity. He works with individuals and organizations, offering a range of retreats and trainings that explore personal empowerment and resilience.

This story explores Rupert's first adventures in the Zimbabwean bush as a young man, and how his perspective toward the non-human world has changed over the course of his life.

BELONGING

RUPERT MARQUES

*"You whose day it is
Get out your rainbow colours
And make it beautiful"*
Traditional Nootka song

I remember as a young boy standing by my bedroom window, looking far over the fields to the distant horizon and wondering what wilds lay beyond. Had I risen up like a bird and actually seen what lay beyond – more miles of monoculture fields and housing estates – something in me would have died. That something, although I could not have articulated it then, was the sense that there existed something vaster and wilder than the human culture I lived within.

As a teenager I felt a strong dissatisfaction with my culture; the "food" of cultural values and narratives that I was being served daily did not nourish me in the way my hungry soul wanted. I was yearning for meaning, for purpose, for knowing something that would bring me to life, rather than dull me. I remember in school not being the slightest bit interested in how many square metres of carpet it would take to fill a particular-sized room, or having to memorize a lineage of monarchs. I was needing to know how we might begin to alleviate the magnitude of suffering we were causing to the wider natural world, how to attend to the vast social inequality that would leave some hungry while others, such as myself, with difficult choices with regard to what flavour of ice cream we would buy. When I observed the adults around me engaged in the routine of nine-to-five work, and then coming back to watch TV to find some semblance of relief, I was not much drawn to the prospects of getting a good (by which was meant well-paid) job. This dissatisfaction, though not easy to live through, was in fact my saviour, for it demanded that I find purpose and not settle for a life lacking in integrity.

In those early years my primary solace was the wider natural world. With my first paycheck I bought a backpack, some boots and a sleeping bag, and journeyed up to Scotland to get a sense of something that lay beyond my culture. I froze my butt off on that first sojourn, yet it was one of my first tastes of being alone in the wild, and seeing what was left when so many of the trappings and amusements of culture were left behind. Thus began my call to undertake solitary journeys into wild places and there to find the space and the time to contemplate the direction and purpose of my life. It was the beginning of realizing in a visceral sense that I belonged to something so much larger than human culture.

This yearning to be immersed in wilderness continued to call me, and in my mid-twenties I felt the draw to be in a landscape that was not at all subjugated by human presence, to feel myself as a human dominated by the land and not the other way around, to experience how it might feel to be part of the food chain. I had grown up in suburban central England with little contact with wild land. Although I had ventured out to Scotland and Wales and wilder parts of England, there was still a sense of the land being domesticated, controlled, not really wild. I wanted to have some sense of how it might feel to meet the wild on its own terms, to see and feel what wilderness really was, and how that might affect me. Little did I realize how soon I was to experience this, and how the reality differed from what I had imagined.

During a course at Schumacher College in Devon, with renowned activist Joanna Macy, I had become friends with a woman from Zimbabwe who was working on revegetating disused mine tailings. On an impulse I wrote to her asking if I could come and visit for some months, with the intention of going out solo into the bush for extended periods, imagining the wild lands of Africa that I had seen from picture books and TV in my childhood. Within a few short months I was viewing a dry African landscape out of a plane window. That bird's-eye perspective was a wake-up call for me as I saw to my dismay that the majority of the land was cultivated or grazed, changed and dominated by human presence. Even here, in the heart of Africa, I thought to myself, the wilderness I had expected no longer existed in the grandeur it once did. Though, as I was later to find out, it was still possible to stand on a high prominence in the midst of Hwange National Park and survey an untamed wilderness stretched out uninterrupted, extending beyond my sight in all directions.

I stayed with Bev and her family in the capital, Harare, for some days, encountering the significant inequality between white and Black people that was more hidden in my own culture, but here much more blatantly obvious yet still accepted as normal. This mindset of domination, whether with regard to race or gender or nation or species (as in the case of humans and the wider earth community), continues to cut right through our collective lives. I cannot envisage a viable future without attending to the internal and external conditions that reinforce this delusion of fundamental separation. Seeing through this delusion on so many levels feels like the crucial work of our times.

Bev's home became the base from which I would journey out to different wilderness locations. My first trip was with Bev, who was travelling to gather seeds from village communities to test whether various species of native plants would be able to grow in the highly polluted mine tailings that were proving problematic to revegetate. After some days of travel and visiting different communities, Bev dropped me off at Hwange National Park in the west of the country, covering a large area of wilderness about three-quarters of the size of Wales. At Hwange it was only permitted to venture out into the bush in a group with an armed escort, but this was not the way I wanted to explore the wilderness, not the experience that I had travelled halfway around the world for. It did not take long before I had scouted out a hole in the fencing that encircled the camp, and at dawn and dusk I would walk out alone into the bush.

As soon as I walked out through the fence line, the change was immediate. Wherever I walked, I walked with the most intense presence, alert to the slightest sound or movement in the bush. I recall on the first day the moment when a porcupine burst forth from hiding in a bush that I had walked by, and I nearly jumped out of my skin, my heart racing as fast as that porcupine. At times fear would dominate my experience; I remember the first time I heard the roar of a lion while out walking. I froze and had to steady myself, and stop myself from running back to the camp. I had no idea that lions don't roar when they are hunting, they are silent then; the sound of the lion's roar simply registered to me as "I could be dinner".

This alertness and awareness of my surroundings was unique to me. I had never experienced that level of awareness of my environment before; I was present with each step and attentive to the slightest sound. This came about through knowing my life depended upon it and allowed no room for complacency. There was simply no room for dwelling absent-mindedly in daydreams or thoughts about the future, there was just the immediacy of presence because it was necessary. What this allowed me to begin to experience was an intimacy, a closeness with the land in a manner I had not encountered before.

Even though the sense of actually being part of the food chain rather than being the dominant species in the environment never left me when out in the bush, it was not always dominated by fear. Although in some moments a visceral fear was present, at other times my experience was more like resting into an alert and yet easeful presence that became more natural as I spent time wandering alone in the bush. I recall feeling so intimate with the land that at one point I had the wish that in old age I would simply walk out and lie down upon that land, offering up my body to that landscape and its inhabitants. I have since changed my mind on this matter and yet something in it still deeply resonates to this day, to offer oneself up at the end of one's days, to be received by the earth that brought one forth.

There was one other significant encounter I had during my time at Hwange, yet this was with humans. Bev introduced me to a couple who had lived in the park for many years, studying and protecting the endangered African wild dog (Lycaon pictus). The African wild dog is the oldest canine on the earth, but now numbers less than 6,000 individuals. In listening to this couple, hearing their passion and dedication, I was deeply inspired by witnessing them offering the majority of their lives to the protection of another species – those beautiful wild dogs, who in all probability would number far fewer today were it not for their work. As I write, I reflect how it might feel, at the end of my own life, to know that another species, or part of a landscape, or a number of people had benefited from my presence here on this earth.

After my time at Hwange, I travelled north to Zambezi National Park, adjacent to Victoria Falls. The vegetation was far denser than at Hwange and forested in some areas. It was here that I had an encounter that firmly reminded me of my vulnerability rather than superiority as a human in that landscape. Again, I had set out alone to explore the land, the huge trees I had no familiarity with, the calls that were new to my ears, and the feeling of being alert and immersed within an environment, rather than complacently passing through it on automatic pilot. Although I had few visible landmarks in that densely vegetated land, I kept some sense of direction from the constant sound of the falls that could be heard from several kilometres away.

At some point in the day I spotted a huge bull elephant with a broken tusk, who was urinating. I watched for what seemed like ages (elephants can urinate for quite a long time, I learned). When he had finished, he began to move off and then noticed me and began to walk slowly in my direction. African bush elephants can grow over 3 metres (10 feet) high and to me it seemed like an animal the size of a house was approaching me. It was a very curious experience as this huge being slowly approached me. Later, I reflected on my experience, and what I felt at that time was somehow similar to how I imagined deer might feel when I had stalked them. I held no harmful intention toward the deer, I just wanted to get as close as I could and observe them, but at some point when I got too close the deer would flee. It was like that for me then, as this bull elephant approached, even though he was showing no aggression. When he got too close I found my body, of its own accord, just started to back away, facing him as I retreated. He continued to approach and I turned around and picked up my pace – and so did he. I began to run, and then I heard this tremendous trumpeting and crushing of vegetation – he was charging me, flattening everything before him. At this point something in me shifted and now I was really running, and for few moments experienced a sensation I had never previously, nor since, encountered: the unique and exhilarating experience of running for my life. I ran zigzag behind the closest big trees I could see, knowing he would not be able to topple them. And then as soon as his charge had started, it stopped; the chase must have lasted for no more than 15 seconds, though I ran for considerably longer than this! Looking back on the experience now, I smile, but at the time I was taken by that visceral experience of being one animal running from another. I was beginning to experience how it might feel to be part of the food chain.

On another occasion I had travelled to Mana Pools National Park in the far north of the country. One of my favourite memories of that time is an evening by a small river watching all manner of animals, including baby elephants, come to take water as the sun began to descend, casting long streams of yellow light through the vegetation amid a rising cacophony of sounds from the bush.

On my way back from Mana Pools, I had an interaction that again reminded me of my place in that landscape, not as the dominant species but rather as a vulnerable visitor to that community. It was a humbling encounter. As I walked back from the river toward my campsite, I needed to cross a large open expanse of grassland, and as I walked out across it, from the other side a water buffalo began crossing toward me. I altered my direction to veer right or left of the buffalo's direction, but wherever I veered, that buffalo altered his path to keep in front of me. As we drew closer, I recall the conversation in my mind: "Look, I just want to get to my camp. I'm not going to walk all the way around this grassland and go out of my way when I can go straight across." I kept going and when we were separated by about 100 metres (330 feet), I remember saying to myself something like: "I'm not going to back down, one of us is going to have to back down and it's not going to be me." At about 50 metres (164 feet) apart I stopped, and so did the buffalo.

"All I want is to just get to the other side. I'm not disturbing you and I'm not going to go the long way around. I'm not going to back down." Then I slowly began moving forward. The buffalo's response to the stand-off was simple and effective; it began pawing the ground with its front hooves. As soon I saw the buffalo pawing the ground, immediately I regained some sense of perspective and humility. There was no way I was coming out on top in this – it was crazy to think I could go head-to-head with a buffalo like it was some domesticated cow in a field in England that I could shoo away. Quickly now, remaining full face on to the buffalo, I began backing away, glad that he had enough patience with me to not charge. I remember on that long walk back around the grassland, smiling to myself, thinking this is what I had wanted to experience after all, to meet the wild on its own terms! I got back just as the light was falling, feeling humbled and grateful to be back before dark.

I was fearful of not returning to camp before nightfall, as the nights did, at times, bring fear for me. One particular night at Mana Pools stands out in my mind. The most eerie sound I ever heard in the bush was that of hyena calls and cackles. That night, in my tent by the river, I was awoken by the calls as they were getting close. I remember ensuring that my knife and headlight were close by me as I lay there, hypervigilant to the calls. Then, as they grew very close, I peeked out to see their shapes prowling around my tent in the light of the moon. Their cries and cackling were intense. The stories of hyenas as a pack being able to take down a buffalo came to my mind. I knew if they did choose to attack, the thin walls of my tent would provide little protection, but that night those walls felt like a fortification to me. I wavered between choosing to shout and shine my headlight through the tent or remaining motionless, hardly daring to breathe. I chose the latter, and in time the hyenas did eventually leave. I'm sure they had my scent but not the sight of me, the thin walls of my tent offering that needed protection. In the morning I scouted around for their tracks and saw many, not only from the hyenas but also an elephant. I had not heard the elephant in the night but it must also have walked by the river. It seems ridiculous now, but my mind conjured thoughts of future nights and the fear of an elephant walking straight through my tent on its way through the bush, my small tent not even an inconvenience for the huge being.

As part of my longing to experience wilderness, I also wanted to spend time with people who lived far more intimately connected to a landscape and its inhabitants than in my own culture. I wanted to understand something of how a relationship with a particular land could make up a central aspect of a community's way of life and their spirituality, as well as the challenges to keep this alive in the face of modernity. My friend Bev had a contact in a small village of the Batonga people, who were originally river-based and forcibly relocated from beside the Zambezi River, their ancestral home, when the Kariba Dam was constructed. It was arranged for me to stay in the compound of a young man who spoke some English and who would serve as my translator. He lived together with his immediate family of wife and child in their own compound, consisting of a few round earthen huts within an area of land fenced off with thorn bush – the area used for growing a few crops and for enclosing their animals. Around them was the compound of their extended family and, further, the compounds of other members of the community. I was given the food store to sleep in – a hut with mud walls and a thatched roof, the door of which was an oil barrel rolled against the opening. This hut I would share with several hundred dried corn cobs. I once tried pounding that dried corn with the huge wooden staves that the women use with such fluidity and grace of movement, involving their whole bodies. It was an embarrassing experience that brought forth laughter from my host and his wife.

During my time with the Batonga people, I learned something about their plight, of how it was to be taken from their land and life-ways, from that which sustained them. The Batonga were a fisher folk and what farming they did depended upon seasonal floods, so when forcibly moved to a dry, poor and stony land their very way of living and providing for themselves was no longer possible. So much of their culture, from their ancestral shrines to their connection with their river god Nyaminyami, was also lost to them. Mostly what I learned from the Batonga about a depth of connection and relationship with the land was the consequences of this connection being severed, and how this creates such a disconnection from the many threads of belonging that actually make up what they would refer to as a healthy person. It seemed to me, as I spoke with members of the community, from what was said and also from the expressions as they spoke, that a life-giving umbilical cord had been cut between the people and their land. I reflect on my own life and my own culture, and how such dislocation from the land and the spirit of the land seems such a common experience, as though we, too, are severed from the umbilicus of that which we belong to, but the difference is that we don't even recognize it. As the poet Lew Welch once wrote, "They have lost it, lost it ... and their children will never even wish for it." How can we remember that which we do not even recognize we have lost?

One encounter in particular during my time with the Batonga people reminded me of how widely divergent beliefs or perceptions about the world can be among people living different life-ways. I was sitting in the compound for the evening meal together with my host and a group of elders, who had come to inquire about what I was doing there. We were conversing through my host the translator, when at one point he asked me a question that I had to ask him to repeat, for what I thought I heard was, "What planet are you from?" He repeated the question just as I had heard it and I replied somewhat perplexed, "What do you mean, which planet?" He then asked the group of elders to clarify, and then told me that the elders often see machines coming down from the sky and so they want to know which planet in the sky I had come from. I remember looking at him to see if he was serious, but his face remained the same. I responded that I live on this planet but come from the other side of it as I mimicked with my hands the sphere of the earth and taking off from one side and landing on the other side. When he translated this, the response from the elders was an uproar of laughter – they found it hilarious that I would speak of the earth as round. I thought on this afterwards, thinking that conceptually I was right, but yet it was the elders who spoke of the planet as we actually experience it, a relatively flat landscape that we live within and are invited to commune with every day. Perhaps this points to the difference I had wanted to understand between a land-based people and my own culture: one thinks about the land from the outside and knows it as an object; the other directly experiences the land from within it and knows it as a subject.

One of the highlights of my time in the wilderness of Zimbabwe was a trip I made to Chimanimani in the far east of the country, an area known for its high, narrow mountain passes. I recall walking up the steep single-track path as I entered the park, a sheer drop to my left and carrying a heavy pack. Part of the reason for the heavy pack was that I had decided I would go simple with my food for the trip, eating raw and taking seeds and nuts and as much fresh fruit as I could carry, particularly bananas. This was the one and only time I tried this – aside from the weight, later in the trip I would find that the inside of my backpack had become a mess of banana smoothie!

At Chimanimani I wanted to go high and remote, away from anyone else and have an overview of the lands surrounding this high terrain. Eventually I made my way to a high plateau and a small cave by a pool. This seemed like such a paradise to me; I had a cave for shelter, enough food, and a pool to swim in and to collect my water from. I made my camp there, high above the clouds. It's hard to describe the sense of tranquillity I felt there; the solitude and simplicity of my days in the presence of this vast and rugged landscape were the embodiment of a dream I had had for a long time. I recall sitting by the cave and pool in the evenings and watching the clouds roll over the valleys below me, their colours turning in the low sun, and the feeling of having finally arrived.

Even though there were many moments of feeling intimate with a particular wilderness and its inhabitants because of the necessity of a heightened level of awareness, it was during a week's solo at a small cabin in a semi-wild landscape that I felt a sense of intimacy with the land that was not born from such a heightened vigilance. I was dropped off at a small rudimentary cabin that had been built by one of Bev's friends, with a week's supply of food in a metal crate and a nearby stream serving as my water source. The cabin was on wild land that was now being encroached upon by small-scale herders from some remote villages. I hardly saw or heard anyone during the week save for an occasional herder. It was the least dramatic and yet most nourishing experience of my whole journey in Zimbabwe. My days would pass simply, rising with the dawn and the great cacophony of animal and insect sounds the new day brought. I would walk to the river to bathe and gather water, prepare simple food and spend my days wandering alone, feeling at ease in the landscape.

The experience of being in the bush at the cabin was a good transition for me. Perhaps because I had the cabin, the sense of being at home mingled with the experience of being a visitor to the land. The gift of that time, the simplicity and slowness of pace, living minimally and yet comfortably, allowed me to reflect upon what aspects of my time in the bush I could take with me into my wider life. It would have something to do with the pace at which I live my life and what I consciously give my attention to during my days. At the cabin, I remember in the evenings as the sun began its descent down to the edge of the world, I would climb up to a high rocky prominence and perch there as the day slowly ended and the light changed across the whole landscape, the hazy oranges turning to purple and indigo, and the sound of the birds calling down the day filling the evening. In those moments life seemed so completely enough. The challenge, however, of cultivating some of the simplicity and attentive presence I had begun to experience in the wilderness back into my wider life within human culture turned out to be far harder than I'd imagined.

––––––––––

Now, some 25 years after my return from Africa, and many travels and experiences behind me, I am in a better place to reflect upon that challenge. I still feel the draw to experience a depth of connection with a landscape, to be intimate with the wider sensuous life, though these days this doesn't centre around the need to feel so directly a part of the food chain. At this time in my life, the invitation is more about finding a daily intimacy or communion with the wider natural world, and how this sits alongside and supports a life engaged with my human community. I still venture out alone to the land, and yet now the majority of my time in the outdoors is given to supporting others in exploring their own relationship to themselves and the natural world through the mirror and refuge of wild places. On reflection, it is no surprise that I am drawn to serve others through the pathways I myself have been touched by; what we love and what nourishes us we are naturally drawn to share with others.

Some of the gifts and learnings I receive now from land and sea are perhaps more subtle and yet no less significant than my adventures of younger years, and they don't require me to travel quite so far from home. One of the gifts I'm often reminded of has to do with stillness, with receptivity. As I write, I'm sitting on a huge granite boulder at the foot of the sea on the Cornish coast, the sun lighting up the water, a few solitary birds wheeling in the white-grey sky, the sounds of the water undulating and washing over the smoothly rounded rocks. All of this inviting my presence, and there is nothing I have to do save receive. In a culture of constant doing, it goes against the grain to pause, to let things be, and through this to allow life to flow into one, to find a home within oneself. This stopping that's so counter-cultural requires something to support us if we are to go against the grain of our conditioning. The wider natural world is a faithful companion in this regard, inviting us to receive life, rather than be constantly "doing to" life, as though our life were one long to-do list to be completed day after day. Perhaps life itself is ceaselessly trying to catch up with us, and if only we would just slow down and pause, it could find us again.

Being beside this vast sea stretching out all around, I feel my own smallness; how the life that holds me is so much larger than me. There is something deeply liberating in seeing the smallness of our lives against a far larger ground. In seeing life this way, my own thoughts and worries take on their rightful size; they don't have to fill the entire space of my mind as is their habit. The land invites me into a conversation brought forth in the language of clouds and grasses and waters, offering respite from the familiar repetition of personal narrative churning around my mind. It is a relief, releasing the tight grip of the mind and opening to a conversation, a relationship, that is always about what is here now.

After immersing myself naked in these cold, clear, springtime waters, I find myself shivering a little in the stiff breeze. The feeling of being held by the water as I swim over the smooth rocks and seaweed, eyes wide open to the unique colours and forms within that watery realm is one of being fully embodied in communion with this sensuous world. I do not last for long in that cold blue-green realm, but the experience reminds me how it feels to inhabit this animal body, how it feels to experience life through a sensory relationship with the world – it is an embodied aliveness. This aliveness is what the land and waters continually invite us to remember. The challenge, I find, is for this embodiment to flow into my everyday life while living in a human-dominated world. It's not easy and the distractions are many, and yet even in the midst of our busy cultural lives the sensuous world still beckons, can break through like dandelions emerging through concrete, inviting us back into an embodied participation with life. Sometimes it's through the cracks that we encounter what lies underneath the surface of our lives.

There have been moments, even here amid the beauty of the Cornish coast in springtime, when I have gazed at the sea and thoughts have arisen unbidden of the desecration of the oceans within my own lifetime: large areas of seabed trawled and degraded, whole ecosystems of marine life that once flourished and are now desecrated, the pollution that daily washes into these very waters and the abundant plastic waste that is scattered upon this shoreline. Over the years I've found that seeking refuge within a landscape is not just about moments of tranquillity or ease – a true refuge has to hold me in times of descent as well as ascent. The land is where I go when I'm in my grief, when the world seems too heavy, too painful and I need solace. Invariably, when I'm in my own descent, when I'm dragged down by the voices of inadequacy or shame or confusion, when I'm not able to hold myself, I will go out to the land, for it holds me when I cannot. The land does not demand anything from me but welcomes me as is, including my brokenness. I remember once walking up an old hill in Somerset after a particularly painful time, feeling the taste of unworthiness thick inside me, and in my defeat lowering my head to the base of a huge oak tree. The weight of my head on the rough texture of bark merged with the heavy, raw feelings inside me. After a while I raised my head and looked up, the green fields and hills stretching to the horizon, the pale sky meeting that horizon … and nothing happened. Nothing happened save that I was held, like everything in creation is held, not a single thing out of place. This is grace, knowing that we are met, are held, not because we have finally attained to some ideal, but that right here in the midst of our imperfection we are not cast out, abandoned, but are held. Only our forgetting covers this up. The land reminds us when we forget, it does not forget.

As the dusk draws on, I'm noticing the light draining out of the day, the shadows lengthening over the water, the clouds darkening, the breeze becoming colder. There are moments like these when I'm taken in a visceral sense by the fleeting nature and inevitable passing away of things. To see that everything we have done, all those we love and all that is precious to us will pass, and that at length we will lose everything, is a hard truth to come close to, and when we do it pierces us. I find, though, that this is not a truth that invites depression but rather one that tenderizes me, has the power to break through my complacency, my taking life for granted, opening me to the preciousness of this life, precisely because I know it will fade. The ceaselessly shifting movements that are the very fabric of the wider natural world remind us, if we are attentive, that the moment does not last long, that each day passes and will not come again.

Now, above in the evening sky, against the pale blue, white folds of clouds are floating, tinged yellow on their underbellies by the low sun. In such moments, when I'm simply present, when I'm not looking for a better moment, I find my place, I come home, and what is before me is at last able to enter me. It's such grace, to be reminded that it is in the ordinary, not the extra-ordinary, that what I'm looking for is to be found. It seems at times so far away, and yet the possibility is ever present, when our eyes are "unclouded by longing" as they say in Zen. This sensuous world is ceaselessly offering itself to us – the birds, the clouds, the waters, the insects and grasses inviting us toward intimacy – but we are not so ceaselessly receptive, we are often "inattentive to wonders" as poet Walt Whitman once remarked. Being here, I'm reminded that it is the quality of awareness itself that opens us up to the preciousness within the ordinary, and that this awareness does not depend upon a lion's roar or an elephant's charge. The land and the sea are always inviting us toward presence, and perhaps presence itself is one of the most precious offerings we in turn make to the land, to the sea, and in making this offering, we ourselves find our home.

That same call to know wildness from my youth, when looking out of my bedroom window, is still alive in me. The difference now is that I know there is as much landscape within as without, and both must be known, both must be tended to. And also this, that from a larger perspective there is just one seamless landscape knowing itself, touching its own face, wondering at itself. In this we find our deeper belonging, our larger identity, and recognize, as psychologist James Hillman observed, "The greater part of the soul lies outside the body."

As I close this chapter, I reflect on the individual, social and ecological suffering we are collectively living through in these times, the larger narrative our lives are bound up with. To be disturbed is a sign we are living consciously, and yet there is such need to balance this disturbance with what nourishes us, with remembering our deeper identity. To be in an intimate relationship with the wider natural world reveals both the wounding and the beauty; we are embedded in both, and both serve to mature our hearts. Over many years of being disturbed, I've come to live with the understanding that it's far beyond my personal agency to bring about the change I want to see in the world, and yet at the same time I also realize that my own contribution is necessary. My response to the disturbance, all that is left for me, is the responsibility and the privilege of offering my own life into an uncertain future. Each of us is significant, each of us has a purpose in the brief window of time we walk upon this earth to offer our lives into the larger collective tapestry and, in some small way, make life more beautiful because of our presence. Through this we become a good ancestor to all those human and non-humans yet to be born, yet to receive the precious gift of a life on planet earth.

The day is coming to an end once again, the sun glimmering over the sea, turning it white, the air becoming cold, and all around me the sound of birds singing down the day.

ORANGE SAVANNAH

CHLOÉ DYSON

I am the African Savannah,
we met when I was young.
Heart burst open. Eyes like oranges
peeled of their waxy lids
reconfigured with translucent skins – as if
portals to a different plain.
Where people and the wildebeest roam
uninterrupted. Silhouettes of kudu and
single trees.
Un-ending equilibrium.

"We could be the African Savannah"
~ A blistering orange speaks in the sky.
Natural order restored into segments,
each species inhabiting its juicy and delicious
slice. Compressed – extended synchronicity – with
their neighbour's niche, and their neighbour's
niche and their neighbour's niche
fanning on and on into
one concertinaed
imperfect whole.

We are the African Savannah.
The taste: electric, wild, natural, complete.
The smell: sweet, sharp, bloody, alive.
The texture: rugged, untamed, arid and
everlasting. The unshakable seed,
now buried in a modern container – like the forgotten
orange left languishing in the depths of a smooth
white, ceramic fruit bowl.
Planted when I was young –
eaten daily.

Orange Savannah © Chloé Dyson, 2023

**After moving to Stroud, UK, to campaign
for Stop Ecocide, Chloé began to explore
her connection to nature through poetic verse.
Inspired and held by the landscape, the adventure
has revealed her voice for the earth.**

Denise is a creative practitioner, ceremonialist and experiential facilitator with over 20 years' experience in creating and holding safe spaces for powerful transformation. Her passion is for the deep-embodied remembering that is encoded within our beings using music, dance, prayer and landscape as access points. Denise's work has evolved from many immersions into indigenous wisdom, including the hunter-gatherers of the Cameroonian rainforest, the mbira tradition in Zimbabwe and her own embodied movement practice in the landscapes of Devon, UK.

"Kin" is a creative piece arising from her solo time on the land in Devon.

KIN

DENISE ROWE

I wake. It is still dark.

The song of the sunrise is whispering over the water, this water companion, pottering along, unfazed in the valley. I've been with her for some years now, listening to her, taking time to be at her pace and to hear her wisdom.

She has led me on this journey, with an invitation to face my fears, and step into the landscape beyond them.

And so I am here, in a valley on Dartmoor with a tarp for cover, a sleeping bag for warmth, a bottle that filters the water from this stream and not much else. I am on the fourth of four vision quests. Each quest is three days and three nights without food or distractions or human company: three days and three nights of immersion into the land, with the fire and the water and the non-human beings.

In the last quest I stood and faced a fear.

In the night, the fire had died down and I could hear the call of the stags in the forest, loud and powerful. I felt small. I knew that stags in rut could be dangerous, and I was alone, three days in, weak from not eating but strong from prayers. There was nowhere to hide, no energy in my body to run, and so I stood and I said thank you for this life, thank you for the mystery of it, thank you for the beauty.

In my small self I felt something big, something ancient, something knowing, something alive that is bigger than the version of me that is afraid. And I felt the stag as family, alive and well in the forest, and I gave thanks for all that sustains me.

The stag didn't come. Eventually I sat down. Eventually I lay down. Eventually I slept.

This morning it's cold, cold like the water.

The beech trees and the stag watched me walk down here. This is my fourth quest on the moor; a call for homecoming and wholeness and sovereignty in the old way, the old way that is becoming new to me.

I've been here three days and three nights, with the river and the rowan trees as company.

It is good.

When I first thought about questing, I was afraid, worried about the hunger and the dark and the aloneness. Now I'm understanding we are never alone. We are woven as part of one big family, with so many friends to lean into.

This morning the light is coming to join us, me and the rowan and the river.

"Breathe this in," she says.

Nothing is happening.

Breathe this in.

It can be simple like this. It can be beautiful like this. All of the troubles and questions can fall away like this, fall away into the river to be resolved within the water and emerge fresh as gateways and growth.

The rowan, forerunner, courageous and generous, says:

"Stand tall
Be the signpost
Trust."

I'm starting to understand trust, that trust is a choice, and the only deal that life is striking. Trust, because it won't all be made clear and the path will only be revealed one step at a time.

This is not a trust that I will get what I thought I needed, or that things will pan out as I hoped they would. It's a trust in something bigger that's holding us all, that there is a way to be found if I follow the way of the water, a way of effortless aliveness, a way of peace.

These quests are bringing me home. Home to the simplicity of being alive, home to my relationship with earth and sky, fire and water, home to gratitude, home to prayer.

It's six months later.

I am running. My busy mind is grappling with the complexities of it all; planning, rehearsing, trying to make sense and bring things into order.

And the river says:

**"Quiet mind now
Do you hear me pour through
Making valleys
In this body of yours
You are carried
There's nothing you need to be waiting for
Quiet mind now."**

And the fire says:

**"Quiet mind now
Do you hear me roar through
Making mountains
In this body of yours
You are standing**

There's nothing you need to be hiding for
Quiet mind now."

And the earth says:

"Quiet mind now
Do you feel me here
True and steady
In this body of yours
You are ready
There's nothing you need to be waiting for
Quiet mind now."

And the air says:

"Quiet mind now
Do you feel me here
True and open
In this body of yours
You have spoken
There's nothing you need to be hiding for
Quiet mind now."

I can't harvest all of this at once. I can't tell you all of this neatly as one individual story with a beginning and a middle and an end. It's not like that. It's woven. We are woven of one another, an interwoven web of kin, each holding pieces of the puzzle, each with our paths to tread.

The water speaks to me of kindness, a kindness that goes beyond what my mind can understand. She asks me to open to it, this kindness. She asks me, again and again, to trust.

And it's like that, the same message is brought to me again and again. When did these teachings begin? Maybe in the woods of my childhood, when I couldn't find my belonging with the humans, when I sought refuge from the bullying and the prejudice.

When did these voices become louder? Maybe in the Cameroonian rainforest with the Baka hunter-gatherers. Maybe it was that moment when I asked for a lesson in dance and the only way to give me that lesson was for the whole tribe to gather in ceremony at full moon, to sing and dance in the moonlight. The message was clear: it's not possible alone, it's not an alone thing.

I am running. And every step is my willingness to stay with this.

I am running among kin, asked to drop my demands, my conditions on life, the expectations that keep my life narrow and get in the way of me receiving what is being offered here.

This is a different kind of kin, uncomplicated. Here we are, all in this together. It doesn't mean it's easy. It means it's big and beautiful.

I am running and it brings me out into my family, out of my limited human world into something wider. The relief of it floods my spirit as a remembering.

I am running, even though I didn't feel like it, even though I woke feeling tired and had all kinds of reasons not to. Here I am. Because I know something bigger than the stories of my mind, and for this knowing I give thanks to the non-human beings who have expanded my horizons and my ability to let life in.

I am running. And every step reminds me that I can take one step at a time, and every breath reminds me to feel the journey and not focus on the ending.

I am running and I find myself with cedar trees. I rest my body into their folded skin, into their height, and pray with them, drinking in their scent. Smells evoke memories. The smell of the cedar evokes the memories of my ancestors from various lands at various times. And here we are together again, the same message: kin.

I am running and I reach the river. With the water I pray for integration into wholeness, for the remembering of ourselves as kin.

The water is cold. I know she is cold. She doesn't get warmer. It's not about that; it's not about seeking comfort. It's about getting comfortable being with what is.

There are so many processes simultaneously unfolding. It's a mystery. And the water pours through it all, vital and effortless, holding us all together, including all of the beings in her expanse, keeping us all alive.

I am learning from her.

I am running. Uphill now. It's harder. And that's okay. The agreement wasn't that this was going to be easy. The agreement was that this was going to be rich and that I was going to be woven in amongst it all, inseparable, belonging.

I am running and I reach the rowan tree at the top of the hill. Rowan, forerunner, signpost, calls us into the magic, calls us along a path woven of sunlight, saying:

**"Stand and breathe in the air and
know you are alive."**

Almost home, and the oak says:

**"Family
Softly family
Kindly family
Always family
Kin."**

GOLD FROM THE STONE

LEMN SISSAY

Gold from the stone
Oil from the Earth
I yearned for my home
From the time of my birth

Strength of a mother's whisper
Shall carry me until
The hand of my lost sister
Joins onto my will

Root to the earth
Blood from the heart
Could never from birth
Be broken apart

Food from the platter
Water from the rain
The subject and the matter
I'm going home again

Can't sell a leaf to a tree
Nor the wind to the atmosphere
I know where I am meant to be
And I can't be satisfied here

Can't give light to the Moon
Nor mist to the drifting cloud
I shall be leaving here soon
Costumed, cultured and crowned
Can't give light to the Sun
Nor a drink to the sea
The Earth I must stand upon
I shall kiss with my history

Sugar from the cane
Coal from the wood
Water from the rain
Life from the blood

Gold from the stone
Oil from the earth
I yearned for my home
From the time of my birth

Food from the platter
Water from the rain
The subject and the matter
I'm going home again

From *Gold from the Stone* by Lemn Sissay,
Canongate Books, 2016.

Lemn is a BAFTA-nominated and award-winning poet,
playwriter, broadcaster and speaker from the UK. He is
also the chancellor of the University of Manchester.

Originally trained as a geologist, Karen is a keynote speaker, flow coach, adventurer and author, and is passionate about supporting others to find "inner gold". Left paralysed by a life-changing accident, she went on to win gold in Rio 2016 in the sport of hand cycling, as part of the British Paralympic team. This led to Quest 79: a project encouraging people to step out of their comfort zone and discover passion, purpose and strength.

This is Karen's story of how the Scottish and Chilean landscapes offered her a crutch during a difficult period of her life.

PATAGONIAN REBOOT

KAREN DARKE

I had been pushing hard for eight years. Thousands of hours and kilometres had been committed to the process of fine-tuning my body to perform on a world-class stage. I had unwaveringly committed to the training plan set by my coach. Throughout the process I had been fortunate to bring home a silver and a gold medal from two Olympic experiences – the London 2012 and Rio 2016 Paralympic Games.

I say "fortunate" because as hard as one tries, I believe a successful outcome is most likely when there is alignment in the mix. Alignment is different from luck. When things work out best it always seems that a beautiful synergy and synchronicity occurs between action, values, intuition and being truthful to ourselves. It leads to a kind of magic.

After Rio, I found myself feeling completely misaligned.

My body was out of whack. My left shoulder wasn't functioning well at all and I was lacking energy. I lay in my apartment for days with the curtains closed and my battery flat. I had nothing to give out into the world. The few watts of energy I had left felt barely enough just to get through the basics of daily survival. For a few weeks all I could do was dress, wash, eat, rest, repeat and just about care for myself. I didn't even feel like I could talk to or see anyone, no matter how good a friend or how much love there

179

might be. I was completely empty. I was scared. I had never felt so vulnerable or so conscious of a cap on my ability to function. The focus required, in those years of training seemed to have taken a toll. I had lost focus elsewhere and also overridden some significant life events in my drive to train and compete and make a success of being a Paralympic cyclist. Retrospectively I can attribute a number of accidents and unexpected surgeries to a mixture of impatience and my propensity to live life full in and full on.

"It's like you've lived ten lives in one," friends often say to me. "Do you ever relax?" "I do," I offer, but without further insight. I like a full life. I see it as a multidimensional jigsaw and love to play with permutations of how all the pieces can fit together in the most effective way possible. None of us need to explain our choices about how we live.

The run up to Rio and "Project Gold" had been a tad too full. Only ten months out from the Paralympic Games, I took myself rather quickly from hospital back to the bike. I needed internal surgery to drain a giant abscess that had accumulated somewhere off my bowel. It wasn't a pleasant procedure and an inconvenient interruption to the winter training programme designed to have me peak in the summer of 2016 for the Rio Paralympics.

"Are you sure you're not pushing yourself a bit hard," a friend commented as I returned from a six-hour ride up in the Mallorcan mountains. I shrugged off their question. I was just doing what I loved and felt happy to be able to get out again after hospital and surgery.

A vision, clear action and a strong state of mind can take us to wondrous places. It never fails to surprise me what we can accomplish when inner strength appears and fuels us to do things. For example, incredible physical feats like an 'impossible' event, an Ironman everyday for a month, or lifting inconceivable weights through coordinated strength of body and mind.

I had a clear vision for Rio: one big effort to see if it was possible to combine mind and body into winning a gold medal.

I like experiments.

Ten months and a lot of pedalling later, things aligned and the experiment was a success.

The evening after winning the gold medal I was early to bed, resting for the road race the next day. I lay in the darkness of the apartment near the Rio seafront listening to the hum of mosquitoes and smiled. My smile turned into feeling tickled pink. The hard work had paid off. It had been an experiment in aligning all parts of myself mentally, physically and in a broader spiritual sense, too. The mountains had been my church. My bike had been my bible. The gold medal had been my prayer. I wasn't quite sure who God had been, but it felt somehow like nature.

Commitment to a big goal is hard work but an intrinsically rewarding experience: all the neurochemicals that get shot into our system with our curiosity and focus give us a natural high and fuel us further. But it's also demanding on our neural circuitry, and beneath my happiness that evening I also felt the burn from the laser-like intensity of the previous months.

I lay there and drifted to the sound of waves breaking on the Rio shore, but in my mind I was somewhere else, a place far cooler and fresher.

I was in the Outer Hebrides. The Hebrides are separated into Inner and Outer, two island chains that break the run of the Atlantic before it laps onto the shores of western Scotland. They are a place of soul and sea and ancient stone circles, a place to transcend time.

I urged to go there.

Ten days later ...

The ferry had one café with a basic menu: oatmeal, beans on toast, black pudding (a type of sausage) or a full Scottish breakfast. I just ordered a coffee. Simple. No decaf, soya or coconut milk, no syrups or extra fluff, no barrage of extra temptations to resist. Then I settled into a plasticky reclining seat and, despite the whimpers of dogs and babies, sank into a peaceful sleep like I hadn't known for days.

We trundled off the ferry with a handful of cars, the chill wind a reminder that we were sharing the latitude with southern Alaska.

We drove a single-track road, meandering across a flat expanse of brilliant yellow irises, the machair fertile and packed with wildflowers and birdlife. It fell away to clear, pristine sea and glowing white sands of crushed shells. The landscape and its striking shades sent tingles down my spine.

Later we lay on the empty beach but clad in puffa jackets rather than bikinis. Our TV was the sky. I lay listening to the call of guillemots, sandpipers and oystercatchers as they swept gracefully above. I breathed the beautiful clean air deep into my belly, my eyes closed, listening, feeling the sandy earth hard but soothing beneath my upper back.

I wanted to sleep in the trunk of my car. "You're such a student." I could hear my brother's voice, but the thought of yet another hotel after the string of impersonal rooms that had filled previous months felt wearisome. I like simple living. In the trunk of my car I was just metres from the Atlantic waves that tumbled onto the beach and could sleep to their lullaby. I wrapped myself in the baffles of a cosy down sleeping bag, closed my eyes and, even with the throb from my shoulder, fell into a deep sleep.

I had felt pain in my left shoulder ever since tweaking something when training in the gym just before leaving for the Rio Games. I had been flinching with pain with daily chores, and movements as simple as getting in and out of my wheelchair. I had to get the legs chopped off my bed in the Paralympic village so that I could slide over more easily and reduce force on my shoulders. I felt held together with Kinesio tape, the stretchy supportive wide tape that works miracles in the way it relieves pressure on muscles and joints. Despite all the usual strategies of massage, stretching and tape, my shoulders were still complaining.

"You have the shoulders of an 80-year-old," the consultant had informed me just a few days before leaving for the Hebrides. "Grade four arthritis."

"How many grades are there?" I had enquired.

"Four. Your shoulder joints are badly worn. Osteoarthritis."

It was a word I didn't like, something I linked to age and decline. A word powerful enough to invoke fear.

"There is also a fragment of bone dislodged that is sitting in the joint." He pointed to the X-ray where I could see a white chunk in the space between the shoulder girdle bones. "And this other white area here is a piece of cartilage that has broken off. These floating pieces of bone and cartilage could be cleaned out with surgery to help reduce the pain and help your mobility."

I had demanded incredible work from my shoulders. From a mechanistic view, it wasn't surprising they were in such a state. Hard work, friction, wear and tear, cells degrading.

"You need corrective surgery, and probably a shoulder replacement at some point," he concluded.

What would I do without my shoulder function?

"Why don't you just relax. Lie on a beach and recover for a month?" my brother urged.

"Take it easy for a while. You've been pushing for years," another well-meaning friend said.

I could see their point.

However, I have learned that total rest is often not the formula for recovery of the body. Also, the thought of lying on a beach held no appeal for me whatsoever. In between Paralympic training sessions, I had lain around for months on end, embracing the importance of recovery. After months living between hotels, from qualifying races to Manchester training to the pre-Rio team "holding camp" in South Wales to a few weeks in the Olympic village, I was absolutely done with lying around.

I had been doing the same things in familiar places for far too long and I felt the need to break out from old routines. I had found competitive cycling fun for a long time, but it was beginning to feel stale and unhealthy.

The short time in the Outer Hebrides and the time connecting with nature restored me with a sense of perspective and balance. Watching the sea rise and fall on the west coast of Lewis and Harris reminded me of the natural process of change, of shifting tides and new directions. Lying on the machair looking up at the clouds blowing across the expansive moody sky, I noticed the simultaneous drama and peace. Curlews and sandpipers played as I breathed deep into my lungs the aromas of grass and flora, and felt the solid support of the wild sandy lawn beneath me.

The patterns and processes that cycle in nature echo into us. Just as oceans roll waves onto a shoreline, nature flows ripples through us.

I returned feeling better than I had for a long time. Although my shoulder was still discombobulated, my time in the timeless Scottish islands felt healing. Simply connecting with wild spaces and natural rhythms is powerfully curative. Whenever I lose balance and perspective in everyday life, immersion in a wild place has consistently been beneficial. It acts as a healing balm for body and soul.

I went on to book a date for shoulder surgery for late December, but I felt resistance to it. I didn't want to be butchered. It would be more trauma, another thing to heal.

Fortunately I had another option lurking, something to try before committing to the knife. Unsurprisingly, it didn't involve resting on a beach.

The potential for "POD" – Post-Olympic Depression – is a well-known risk amongst athletes. With my friend and cycling teammate Steve Bate, along with his wife, Caroline, and another teammate, Jaco van Gass, we had hatched a recovery plan to mitigate the risk of POD. Our idea was to cycle through the wilderness of Patagonia, almost 1,500 kilometres (932 miles) along the largely dirt trail of the Carretera Austral. It begins in the coastal town of Puerto Montt in Chile and follows the Pacific coastline southward toward the Torres del Paine National Park.

I feared that my shoulder might be too far gone to cooperate, but spoke to them about the difficulties I was having. In the state I was in, I was uncertain about being fit enough for the job of cycling and camping in the wilderness of southern Chile.

"We'll help you if you need it," they reassured me. With their positive response and support, I felt encouraged.

We were on.

A month later, I felt the typical mix of scared/excited as we packed and left for Chile.

We ride south, the sun lighting our faces and a crown of mountains glimmering above turquoise rivers and lakes. It is all we heard of and dreamt about. Chilean Patagonia is a region of immense beauty, a vast natural wonderland, a more colourful, vibrant, living version of the Paramount cinema logo. The expansive open mountainscape only hides when we plummet into forest. Then our passage is draped instead by the most enormous leaves, as if in a garden of giants. The scale and diversity of the landscape stuns me. It seems like forest and skies stretch to infinity.

The kilometres and days merge into a time–space continuum. The only punctuations are pauses to sleep and eat, and unexpected moments when we turn a corner to find even greater breath-stealing beauty.

The villages are hundreds of kilometres apart. To ensure we have food and water, we have calculated the number of days between resupply, and stocked up for each section. Our staple morning fuel is oatmeal with *dulce de leche*. The addictive caramel-sugar combo comes in kilogram bags and gives us a daily sugar rush that lasts for hours of pedalling.

The traffic is sparse enough that we can mostly own the road, choosing which rut to follow, picking a course to dodge the deepest gravel or bumpiest sections of road. In many sections the resonance of trucks has turned dirt road to washboard and we are rattled to our bones pedalling over it. I feel grateful that we were able to experience a quieter, wilder Patagonia than will soon arrive when the roads are topped in asphalt and traffic will inevitably follow.

It feels so good to be living with the rhythms and aromas of nature once again. For all the comforts offered by our modern world, I can think of no substitute more satisfying than lying on the grass watching a sinking sun after a day moving through the great outdoors, listening to the soothing bubble of a nearby stream and the crackle of a small fire.

Prior to Patagonia my life had been tending toward more urban living than I'd ever known. Project Gold had required consistent routines to optimize sleep, nutrition and recovery. Breaking that performance routine by hopping away to wild camp for a few days would likely compromise the next race. My adventure and camping days had consequently dwindled, not helped by the requirements of WADA: the World Anti-Doping Agency. It demanded me to report my whereabouts every single day and night. It's not acceptable to report your whereabouts address as "A Tent, Wild Campsite, Wilderness, Chile" with no postcode or specific location. Instructions from UK Anti-Doping were to send a location and coordinates from my mobile phone every night. You can imagine my response.

"No!" While I respect that anti-doping requires some rules, I wasn't going to limit my life to being at a registered postcode. As soon as I reappeared in WADA testing territory at a UK airport hotel, my door was hammered on at 5.30am by officials wanting my blood and urine.

For too long, the natural world had been replaced by a manmade one, my body and brain bathed in plastic, concrete, radiation and climate-regulated environments. From British Cycling's training labs to the delights of an Ibis Budget hotel in downtown Manchester, I had stressed my body training and then stressed it more by breathing dirty street air and watching boxset series on my laptop. After hard training my brain was too fried to concentrate on anything more productive or to be creative. Without that, I was starting to lose my sense of greater meaning and purpose.

I believe in the positive impact of sport, but on a day-to-day basis I felt reduced into a microcosm of tiny circles. I had been fortunate to travel to some far and beautiful locations with the team, but it's incredible how one hotel room can start to feel like any other, be it beside the Italian Dolomites or the Australian coast. My inner spark was slowly fading and hence the lustre of all these places was, too. Our inner world creates our outer, and as I dimmed inside so did the world around me, to the point that I would lie in hotel rooms chastising myself for not appreciating experiences like I should. I was fortunate and proud to be representing my country. I was doing what many would love to: travelling the world living a dream, but it had morphed into a continuum of airports, road trips, hotel rooms and race circuits around industrial estates, with only distant views of mountains. I had to rest when not training, and the air-conditioned hotel rooms started to feel like luxury versions of a prison cell.

My life in high performance sport had become a dichotomy. On the one hand, I had the luxury of time outdoors, riding my bike doing an activity I loved in beautiful places, my focus on an incredible global event that took place every four years. On the other hand, the performance focus required me to spend a lot of time indoors resting so that I would be recovered enough for the next training session. I felt more disconnected from nature than ever in my life, but also detached from other parts of my life. Social events usually didn't fit with a training and racing calendar, so joining friends for a weekend away or family for a special event were often not possibilities I could make a reality.

My connection with other living systems had gradually shrunk. I had begun to feel isolated and lonely.

———————

Among the gravel and the grind of Patagonia are many wonders. Everything is super-sized; trees reach for the clouds, valleys yawn wide and long, leaves cast shadows big enough to shelter under. The bumblebees are obese.

After rattling along the Carretera for 370 kilometres (230 miles), we come to the small village of Puyuhuapi, the forest broken by a disarray of colourful timber houses and shops on the edge of a fjord. We fill our stomachs and souls with giant portions of homemade cod and chips, bread and salad. At Manuela's there is one set menu, to be eaten with a view over the small harbour and the Christmas tree in the village square. The warm evening sun is a reminder that we are in the southern hemisphere, a little different from the previous Christmas when, wrapped up in sweaters, we had hatched the idea to be in Patagonia. It seemed an age ago, the year absorbed by the intensity of training and racing, the uncertainty of making Paralympic selection. The escape to Patagonia is exactly the tonic we all need. The lack of pressure is palpable and I am relearning how to live without it.

Watching the sunset over the lake, I think about how slowly yet quickly we humans adapt to changes in our environment. Like landscapes. In a few years when the asphalt spreads, Puyuhuapi's character will morph. More people will come. More traffic will pollute. Maybe nature will become less super-sized. The price of development. For now, though, Patagonia has something pristine and unique. I can feel it breathing life into me again.

At first it seemed impossibly far to reach Coyhaique, the regional capital, halfway along the Carretera. Two weeks in we have ingested a lot of dust and are getting close. Our day begins in a grassy clearing with the sounds of flapping tents, wind whispering in tall trees, exotic bird call and the rush of a bulging turquoise river. We ride through a wide rolling valley splashed with lilac lupins and yellow gorse, the occasional peak of a high white summit glistening bright against a flawless blue sky. Any delusions of having arrived in heaven are soon ground away by a joint-labouring climb. It's curious how far 14 kilometres (8¾ miles) seems when the road goes relentlessly up and your limbs are weary; when a steep gorge flanked with high walls takes away the horizon; when you feel you are cycling a road so sticky it could be smeared in *dulce de leche*.

The others are spread up the road ahead of me, a relay team in formation, ready to hop off their bikes and turbo-boost me up the hill. It's not what I had imagined or wanted, this dependency on my friends to manage the steep or slippery hills. But I feel grateful for them and the way we have found to journey together, with our different physical challenges and circus of bikes and trailers.

Steve is riding a fat bike, the wide tyres soaking up bumps and potholes and compensating for his limited vision, my wheelchair precariously balanced on a trailer behind him. Jaco had struggled to ride down the first hill we encountered, the massive weight on his trailer tricky to control with one arm of carbon. Caroline is physically intact though not so well trained as the rest of us and she balances a full load of panniers on her bike, along with pots and pans and washing. The ride is a challenge for each of us in different ways, even before the unexpected need to shove me up hills that my spinning wheel struggles to grip.

In Coyhaique – our last outpost – we eat steak and drink beer and prepare for the next section of our journey.

The rain falls as constantly as the gradient rises, from the moody fjords of Chile toward the expanse of Argentina. We will turn south before then, to the black spikes and ice-crusted peaks of central Patagonia, deeper into what is called Region XI or Aysén. Coyhaique is the last significant town along the Carretera, and now it feels like the real adventure is beginning: the wilder half, the tougher half.

My bike wheels flick the heavy rain like an unruly showerhead, and despite my decent waterproof jacket I feel the drops running across my skin, seeping where they shouldn't. We needed to stop, to make camp before dark, but ironically, despite being fed by the clouds all day, our drinking water is low. I feel thirsty, hungry and tired. And life seems distilled to those simple basics – water, food, rest.

"You feeling okay?" I ask Jaco. "Yep, kind of. There's no choice not to, is there?" There really isn't.

But what is harder, really? An elemental day on the road dictated by the crucial ingredients of survival? Or a day rich in comfort, choice and the crazy stress of our daily busyness? Despite our dry mouths, empty stomachs and weary muscles, I'm sure we all feel the same. There's nowhere else we'd rather be.

I've spent years striving to be stronger, faster and more physically able than I am, but my arms will never match the strength of legs.

Maybe that has left me feeling lesser at times; perhaps it has also led me to my incessant pedalling. I'm nonetheless amazed by what my body sustains. I ask a huge amount of it and it rarely fails my will.

For the journey of the Carretera Austral, I'm asking my arthritic shoulders to pedal me through at least 60 kilometres (37 miles) a day of mountainous, gravelly Patagonian terrain. I revel at the absence of pain or complaint from them, especially given how bad they have been. Something about the place, the people, the nature, is making my soul dance in a way it hasn't been able to for a long time. Here, cycling all day through forests and mountains, camping on dusty roadside verges, in gravel rest stops or small grassy clearings, I feel somehow more vital again.

The days pass and we adapt to moving ever more slowly. The forest becomes woven with lakes and rivers; startling glimpses of turquoise luminosity and rushing current are a surprise for the eyes after the kilometres of gravel and endless trees. I was attracted to the opaque hue of turquoise in my years as a geologist. It's what's called a supergene mineral, formed by water percolating through rocks and oxidizing copper sulphide as it passes through. The copper-laden solution reacts with other minerals and then deposits turquoise. I feel we are being percolated as we trickle through Patagonia, and I imagine we will emerge in a supergene-enriched form.

I like it best when the trees fall away to meadows and big skies, when rises in the road are crowned by white summits, where horizons expand all around and I feel things expand within me as well.

On long journeys with hours of riding, there is plenty of time to think. But mostly I don't. That's part of the attraction. Hours of emptiness are punctuated only by fleeting thoughts.

What a beautiful valley! Is that really only 7 kilometres (4¼ miles) we've done so far today? It must be lunchtime soon ...

Highway hypnosis arrives, like the car journey you can't remember. I quickly find myself in an altered mental state, steering and controlling the bike but with no conscious thinking. I find my mind elsewhere but nowhere. I only emerge from this hypnotic state when something happens that breaks the rhythm of pedalling. A break, a village, an even-more-amazing view or bigger-than-ever leaf.

I barely noticed my thought patterns shifting. Before the trip I had been marinating in fear about the future and the consequences of bad shoulders and the possibility of losing my mobility and freedom and independence. But I notice my thoughts moving out of the shadows and up to the horizons and summits around us, appreciating the magic all around. I notice the way the light plays across the landscape, the flashes of sky mirrored in water, the scent of lilacs and the hum of insects, my senses jolted alive.

I feel like I'm waking up from a long coma.

I forget about my shoulder. It has stopped begging my attention. The further south we ride, the more I feel a load shift. My nervous system has been wired with stress and Patagonia is un-funking it. The Carretera's torturous bumps and gravel empty my mind and time steadily slows. Life is distilled back to basics and invigorated by good energy.

The hours stretch out toward nightfall, and around 9pm we finally trundle through damp mossy forest into town. We gather around the signpost that marks our arrival at the end of the road. We are here, in Villa O'Higgins, on the northern edge of Torres del Paine National Park. There has been solid rain for three days and every layer of clothing is sodden. I feel frozen, hungry and exhausted, but despite the rain that has pooled in my collar bones and dribbled down my chest, besides the cold that has numbed my fingers and disabled my grip, I feel happy. It has been an adventure, a transformational ride in the wilds.

My shoulders are free. I can transfer in and out of my bike with ease. I can dress myself. I can reach and stretch without any flinch or wince.

My complex life has been simplified. A comfortable bed has been replaced by gravel pits beside the trail. Endless choices of food have reduced to oatmeal with *dulce de leche*, and tomato and avocado wraps. Fridges full of fizzy drinks and bottled energy have been replaced with stream water and solar-powered zing. Air-conditioning has turned to wind, hotel rooms to a tent. Wifi has disappeared along with sight of a mobile phone.

I feel exponentially healthier and happier. I feel aligned again, in synch with myself and the world around me.

It reminds me that changing our habits and environment changes our reality. When nature is in the mix, then we get a great big reboot of our operating system.

I have no need for shoulder surgery anymore. Later, I will phone to cancel it.

THE NIGHTINGALES IN CONCERT

LAURIE KING

Under the light of the stars and held by the embrace of dark
trees, we listen.
Listen to the song of sweet simplicity,
a resonant reminder of times gone by,
when the nightingales ruled the skies.

How sad that I compared the sound to a machine,
when I should be comparing a machine to their song.
And, "no, The Nightingales isn't a band name".
The car noises in the background are more familiar.
Planes flickering in the dark,
the metal birds that now rule the skies instead.

But tonight, just tonight – we are here for their concert.
A concert of longing, and loss, and love, and hope.
A story of survival in times of adversity.
A song of reproduction and repopulation,
to drown out the cars.
I feel a stirring inside,
the will to create a life where the birds are my alarm clock,
where the ecosystem is my network,
and where my brain is the only hard drive.

The Nightingales in Concert © Laurie King, 2023

**Laurie is a writer, researcher and facilitator exploring
nature connection and sustainability.**

Celia is a mother, sailor, yogi and crofter.
She sailed her first boat, Ada, to Antarctica
and South Georgia and in the fjords of Chile
in the early 2000s. She then spent several
years living in Chile before taking to the
seas again with her son on their aluminium
sailboat, Selkie. She now lives on the isle
of Eigg in Scotland where she runs sailing
charters on Selkie, offers yoga retreats, and
raises Shetland sheep for wool – bringing
all her passions together.

This is the story of her first sailing expedition
on perilous waters to South Georgia in 1998,
how it helped her heal wounds from the past,
and how it shaped her perspective
going forward.

A LITTLE MAGIC IN THE STORM

CELIA BULL

The din in my ears, pounding my senses, is a great cacophony of wind, waves and a rolling rhythmic diesel engine. I'm feeling sick, tired, overwhelmed and scared. In seeking a little respite from the nicotine-smoke-filled wheelhouse, I've pushed forcefully out through the watertight door to the deck and hunkered down next to the fuel tank breather pipe. There is just enough space here to find dry shelter, though swapping cigarette stench for diesel fumes is a poor improvement. The bile in my belly threatens to rise again but I force it down with some determined breaths.

I squint open my eyes and focus on the layers of white paint that wrap and warp the spherical guard rail. Bracing into my nauseous corner, I allow my attention to become drawn to the ghastly waters framed within a single rectangle of the steel barrier. The good ship *Golden Fleece* lurches to starboard and I find myself staring at foam and seething sea, inches from my boots. With a sickening fairground trajectory, the vessel slews to port on a rising swell and I glimpse sky above an angry jade crest. I loll my head back to rest on the door. I'm relying on no one pushing it open. But really, I'm beyond caring. I shut my eyes and just go with the motion of the heaving ocean.

When last I looked at the GPS, we were somewhere halfway between 52 and 54 degrees south, somewhere halfway between the Falkland Islands and South Georgia. My first big sea crossing! And the way I'm feeling, wishing with every fibre in my body that it would be my last. I know, though, that once we reach South Georgia, we must come back and against the prevailing winds, against the east-going giant swells of the Southern Ocean. How can anything be worse than this sea, here and now, which is supposedly all going in the right and easy direction?

The door bumps open, bumps my head and I shift to allow a green-hued human to stagger out onto the deck. We look at each other balefully. I mutter an apology for hogging the only dry deck space. I hear a grunt as a reply and then the door slams back shut, taking the only upright passenger with it. Perversely, this experience brings me some cheer. I'm less alone in my discomfort, although I'm pleased to be left alone with it. This is not a moment I want to share. I'm careful now to keep away from the door. I can feel a bump growing on the side of my head.

I return my gaze to the patch in front of me. The patterns of foam blowing on the surface are fascinating, like corduroys of spume. By keeping my window of vision confined between the vertical of the stanchions and horizontal of the railing, I'm managing my fear. I can cope with what I see there. It's like I'm watching a TV picture of some deep offshore storm from afar rather than up close and too damn personal. I'm avoiding looking out across all the maelstrom in one sweep of the eye. That is too terrifying. I'm trying to keep a lid on my imagination. I'm all too aware of the tempest. Too sensitive to the improbability of being afloat. I'm telling myself, mantra-like, that thousands of years of design is represented in modern boatbuilding. Nice try, Celia!

It's not the only time I've used a mantra to keep the fear at bay. A year ago, running fast along a coast path in southern Tasmania, I was chanting to myself about saving lives. I was concentrating on my feet then, too, willing myself to speed safely along the stony tree-root trail to raise the alarm for my injured climbing partner.

I'm running again now, this time desperately seeking some help for myself and though my feet are planted leaden on the moving deck, I'm sprinting at full tilt. Rolling down, my boots washed by water rushing up from under the rail, I pose the question "Is this the right place!?"

And then I'm rocking back, the sound of the submerged exhaust breaking free from the wave. As my pitching, surf-riding deck comes up for air, I glimpse something incongruous in my quadrant of sea – a tiny dark dot hovering, dancing across the surface. Then it's gone, replaced by sky as the weight gravitates to my back and my stomach is pressed up against the steel wall. Immediately I'm thinking of hummingbirds – the ones I've seen darting in the gardens of Buenos Aires. Is that possible out here, in the Southern Ocean? How? As the ocean comes back into view, I gaze across the surface searching for this anomaly. There again, tiny and black, literally fluttering, seemingly oblivious and impervious to the gale-force winds and whipped-up frenzy of sea. I've a while to watch it as *Golden Fleece* slides down the back side of a big spaced-out swell, a wave travelling unstopped by land, endlessly orbiting the earth. To me, a landlubber alien in this environment, this mass of moving water is heart-stoppingly terrifying, yet here is a bird not much larger than a sparrow, hundreds of miles from the nearest land, searching for food, as relaxed as a wading bird stalking cockles at low tide.

It's gone again. I stare at the water directly in front of me, trying to see what the bird can see. What food is there out here? My metre of sea looks grey, empty and drowningly deep. I lean forward and look around the corner, past the wheelhouse, past the foredeck to the sea beyond. Rain or spray bites at my face and I close my left eye and screw up the right, enough to peer past lashes and the bridge of my nose. I section off areas of sea and scan for movement or something unexpected, a break in the watery status quo. I cast my gaze out across the liquid horizon abeam of me and then swivel my head aft to trace our wake, and there again encounter this extraordinary and calming sight.

I can keep the bird in view for a little while as we travel away from it, but then it becomes too small a speck in the vastness of the ocean, but my eyes are open now and searching. No longer afraid. I feel curious and excited, disbelieving and distracted.

I push myself up, take a deep breath and yank open the door. Mindful of the high sill, I step exaggeratedly inside and stumble across the room to next to the captain's chair.

"What sort of bird is tiny and black and lives out here?" I ask. "And what is it eating?"

My skipper, font of all knowledge, twiddles a corner of moustache between thumb and forefinger, and with a noticeable French accent announces: "Ah, you 'ave witnessed a storm petrel."

Jerome steps down from the driving chair, reaches for the binoculars, and goes to the door to have a look for himself. He beckons, and I go over to peer outside again, mindful of my stomach. As he scans the rolling horizon behind the boat with practised familiarity, he points, and I start to see other birds, this time huge ones, tracking and gliding in these massive winds and waves. Jerome is pointing out albatross. Here, this one has a grey head, another with Cleopatra-like eyeliner. I recognize a fulmar, an old favourite from my sea-cliff climbing days; it tracks near and then plays with the airflow over the handkerchief of mainsail.

"Ah oui, we 'ave crossed the convergence. Now we are in Antarctic waters and these are full of nutrients."

I'm flabbergasted. The sea has suddenly gone from desert to oasis. There are birds in every direction, like a switch has been turned on. Not flocks, but in among the huge waves, held aloft by the power of the air, are great birds, tacking across the wind, searching for food. I can feel goosebumps rising on my arms. I had no idea. My whole life I've gone around oblivious to the existence of this world. Here, at 50-odd degrees south, hundreds of miles from land, is a richness I could never have imagined possible. The ship starts to undergo a transmutation, to shake itself free from the chrysalis of the ugly rolling metal slug it was a few moments ago in my head, to a vessel of wonder that is capable of bringing me here amongst this alien planet. Don't get me wrong, it's not a miracle worker. I'm still feeling sick but I feel removed from it, aware but not wholly taken up with it. Instead my eyes are feasting on this scene. The birds have taken my fear and flown away with it. Now I'm looking on in awe.

Jerome heads back to the swivel stool, and leans forward to look out of the round, clear window, a spinning piece of Perspex that flings rain and spray away and gives him a clear view of the waves rolling ahead. He flicks off the autopilot and returns to steering over the waves at the right angle, one that avoids knocking the boat down or racing too fast down the front of the wave. There is the odd rogue, breaking turquoise cap whipped up by the strong winds. To me, there looks to be chaos all around, but Jerome sees and feels the patterns in the swell, old and new, and calmly guides the boat along the safest path, as if mapped out in tarmac. He is an extraordinary man, now living on an island on the far west of the Falklands, who has sailed in Antarctic waters for three decades. The BBC has him under contract to skipper film crews in these inhospitable oceans for its TV series *The Blue Planet*. Whether it be camera teams, nature enthusiasts, or as in this October's charter of skiers, he needs crew. In a series of bizarre events, I had been handed his fax number and volunteered my novice crewing services.

Maybe it was the next swell that Jerome had seen from the door that sends him back, or maybe just instinct, but just in time the door shuts before the deck is submerged beneath a roaring rush of crushing wave. Even where I had been sitting is swamped and a little noise escapes my throat. Okay, I'm not quite ready to change my whole life for this.

There's a bookshelf downstairs in the saloon and I'm desperate to read up about the storm petrel and all the other birds. Taking a few deep breaths, I clasp the bannister and carefully make my way down the steps. It's not easy, this! The movement is a little less violent lower down in the ship, but even so. The saloon is deserted – no surprises there. The galley is still tidy though it's an effort to keep it that way and to make food. Luckily not much hunger going on at the moment. I can see some bird books on the shelf but I think better of reaching for it. Reading is not going to be on the agenda today!

Jerome has requested a coffee. He's been at the helm for hours, almost a whole day. Drip-feeding him coffee is a crew task and I'm the on-duty crew. The galley has an Aga stove – well, I think it is. It runs on diesel and has been amazingly reliable. The top is always hot and there is a kettle constantly full and wedged securely in place. Luckily it's just instant coffee and sugar in a small brown-stained coffee mug, easy to make; a manageable task that will hit the spot. I'm cold from my stint outside so I cosy up, bracing myself against the stove for a few moments of extremity warming. I enjoy a few thawing minutes before I feel prickly, too hot, and starting to turn green about the gills. I think I'd better go and give this cup to the skipper and return to the outside world.

I'm feeling fairly stupid. I rushed here, to the Falkland Islands, after the bottom fell out of my world. I'm not really sure what happened. One moment all was fine – well, sort of fine. I'm an acceptably proficient climber on a dream tour of Malaysia and Australia with my boyfriend. The next ten years of life are mapped out by future expeditions to big walls in exotic places. But then I'm phoning family and friends with news of a hideous accident on the Totem Pole in Tasmania. My partner, Paul, was struck by a rock which penetrated his skull, leaving him dangling unconscious and bleeding into the sea at the end of a rope. I hauled him up to a ledge, traversed a thin rope from the top of the rock tower to the mainland, and ran to alert the rescue (you can read about this in *The Totem Pole* by Paul Pritchard – he wrote this while healing, and has since gone on to climb Mount Kenya and cycled across the Himalayas). I didn't realize then that I would never enjoy climbing again, always haunted by the devastation of that day.

It was a doctor who told me I had to tell them. It was about 3am in the morning. I'd managed the 160-kilometre (100-mile) drive from the Tasman Peninsular to Hobart. The first hour of that journey, the radio accompaniment was a deathly diabolical playlist until midnight on Friday the 13th yielded to Valentine's Day; Marilyn Manson rolled over for Whitney Houston power-housing "I Will Always Love You". I passed a few roadkills on the way, the raison d'être for the Tasmanian devil rescue centre, whose sign loomed eerily at some point on the lonely ride. I was an emotional wreck by the time I arrived at Hobart hospital and pulled into what I hoped was free street parking.

I made my way to a reception desk and was ushered to a quiet room in the deserted accident and emergency department. Paul was lying on a gurney. Congealing on the floor under his head was a stalagmite of bright red blood and paler fluid. He was breathing and was such a mess. I was told that the surgeons would be arriving soon – that was the plan. They let me stay with him while the theatre team roused themselves from sleep and made their way from their homes around Hobart for an exacting surgery to save a man's life. That was when one of the team took me aside and gently said that I had to phone his parents: I had to prepare them in case he did not come out of the surgery alive. I don't know how I managed to make those calls. To Jean first, his mum. Then I spoke to Anne, his dad's partner. My sister, Elaine. Then friends. The vigil started.

At some point a kind nurse found me a sofa bed. They have a room in the hospital reserved for nearest and dearest. I must have slept, exhausted. I remember coming to and being hit by a jolt of adrenaline as reality hit. I jumped out of the bed, racing for the door, but my body didn't follow through, back spasming in protest and legs leaden and grudgingly responsive after the night of the rescue. As a result, I grated my ankle over a sharp corner of the metal bedframe, creating more blood to clear up and a scar to this day. He was still in theatre. I sat and waited, shell-shocked. It was now 6am. A familiar face, full of concern and warmth, Jane found me. She'd heard about the accident and realized it must be us. I had met her a few days previously climbing here in Hobart. She worked at the hospital and offered me a home for as long as I needed one.

After a month in Tasmania, Paul was deemed fit to fly by the doctors and we made the many flights home to North Wales. With part of his brain missing, he went straight to hospital in Bangor, then a few weeks later to Clatterbridge, a head specialist unit. Somewhere during that time, I stalled. I behaved erratically, badly, took drugs, did stupid things, lost friends, lost climbing, lost my way. Everything was wrong and all I wanted was to escape. And quite simply, I could. Paul couldn't. For that reason, I went as far away from it all as I could, and as far away from everyone I knew and who knew us, who knew me. Even now, thinking about it, the white noise starts. My ears are ringing so I force myself back into my present, focus and stare fixedly through the salt-caked window at the Southern Ocean.

Where are you, dainty storm petrel delicately catching nectar from the waves? Those minute specks of fodder, plankton not plastic I hope, as intoxicating as Nelson's grog. I'm intrigued and fascinated, the petrel pulling at my heart strings. It may be tiny but not frail. It gave me hope that I, too, could not only weather this storm but find sustenance in its embrace. Who knew that a little black-brown bird with a white belly band would be my hero?

Storms pass, as did that one. All the passengers emerged, with everyone ravenous. The crew and the chef were back on duty, preparing delicious food for the table. There's not time to stop and relax until the night watch. That's where I am now. It's 2am and dark as black velvet. Everyone is asleep except me. The radar shows dots that fade and reappear somewhere else on the screen. No shadows pinpointing icebergs. This far south I can expect to see them and it's my turn to keep watch for them in the middle of the night. I have the bird book with me and I make myself a nest on the sofa in the wheelhouse, radar in view, curl my feet up under a blanket and start to read, all eager to learn about the storm petrel that has bedazzled me by its defiance and audacity. The timer is set for a few minutes to bring me out of my book to check on the instrument panel and take a look out of the windows. All is well at sea tonight.

It turns out, so I am told in the first few pages, that this brave little creature that inspired me and lifted me out of my fear, has had many names, mostly dark and devious: Mother Carey's chickens, bird of the devil, satanique – harbingers of terrible things as they flew down the first waves of an arriving storm. I am at first dismayed, then angry, and finally with the injection of a humourless laugh, cynical. These birds, like the sea witch they fly with, do not bring the storm. They are at ease within it and sensible to the storm's nature. I keenly feel my disappointment; how often, as a woman, my role models and inspiration are at times vilified. Earlier this year I had helped organize an international women's climbing symposium. One of the subject areas I was keen to explore was the contradictory language engaged for male and female mountaineers. Alison Hargreaves had died on K2 in 1995 and the vitriol hurled at her cut to the quick of every female climber. Listening to the women present at the meet, it was enlightening to realize that these attitudes were something predominately Western and peculiarly British. The Indian climber Bachendri Pal was celebrated for being a mother and summiting Everest. Different people and different cultures intuit different qualities. As for me, coming up against the ugly brick wall of misogyny makes me dig in my heels, lock horns and get really stubborn, be it women on mountains, women at sea, witches and others in cahoots with the devil.

Wrapped in the cloak of night, the radar a cauldron of unnatural green, flickering shadows, ghosts of movement, I imagined the little brown bird out on the waves, and the true magic of what she is doing to survive, one wave at a time, and I'm determined to do the same.

I spent six edifying months plying the waters between the Falklands, South Georgia and the Antarctic Peninsula. I beheld a pod of nine bow-riding minkes; communed with spy-hopping humpbacks; glided by cathedrals of icebergs sporting congregations of crab-eater seals; looked on aghast as blood-frenzied leopard seals murdered amid a river of royal penguins; sung lullabies to miles of fluffy teddy-bear chicks and their black-and-white parents; sat beside huge smiling albatross and peered stealthily round rock ledges at their slighter sooty cousins. It was easy to slip politely between sunbathing elephant seals lying cheek by jowl along the sandy South Georgia shores – but after Christmas, beware! The beaches and tussock foothills are ransacked by the new year fur-seal patrols – rottweilers on steroids.

All these huge experiences imprinted on me: true wonders of the world that I am so blessed to have witnessed and wandered among, but one tiny little bird sang to me the most, early in that seafari. In the immensity of raw nature, something so small had the courage to survive, a wisp in a Leviathan world. It gave me the courage to stay the course and I enveloped myself in that.

That was almost a quarter of a century ago. The flight of the storm petrel led me a merry dance. Six months after our first encounter, I sold my house, bought a boat and sailed back to the Falklands. I called her Ada, and against the odds I survived my adventures aboard that vessel. I never went back to climbing, though my love for the mountains and beautiful places is as strong as ever. Instead I allowed myself to explore nature by way of water. I have a son who I raised on a boat and, finally, I found a home on the Isle of Eigg in Scotland.

It's easy to look back to the woman I was when I came face to face with a storm petrel and see what a mess I was emotionally. It's harder to admit that I'm still a little messy from time to time. I do well and I'm a fighter, but there are moments I find myself in free fall. Being older, I can recognize the signs and try to ease up on myself, but those close to me – my sister, my son, a few friends – they are the ones who get to deal with me when I'm bouncing around on the rocks at the bottom of my mind. I chose a life surrounded by nature because there is always some wonder, however small, to remind me of the brilliance of life. However difficult my struggle, a fearless storm petrel, a puffin emerging from its burrow, or a tiny wren nesting in the shed, will conjure wonder and hope. Nature has a way of rescuing me every day when the abyss is too close.

For seven years now, I've been running sailing charters amongst the beautiful isles of west and north Scotland. It is home to many seabirds and marine mammals. I love these waters and hope that during my trips I impart this passion to those journeying with me. I have found a home on the Isle of Eigg. Its recent history of the community buyout of the island and its reliance on green energy resonates deeply with my social and ecological ambitions. Eigg folks also know how to have fun, which I need to be reminded to do from time to time... On this isle I tenant a small patch of agricultural land, a croft. My boat anchored me to the seabed and now the croft gathers me to the land itself. I try to give back something, share, and enable others to undertake their own journeys of exploration in nature.

It's dusk; there's a suggestion of orange, so slight in the heavy grey sky that it could be my imagination. The body of water has a luminescence about it. Selkie, my aluminium yacht, is anchored in the sound by Handa Island. The tide is high, and the birds are at eye level. I'm waiting for my guests to return from wandering around the isle. All are in awe of the wildlife we have encountered around the Shiants, Lewis, Skye and Sutherland. It's not been the best forecast – complicated, to say the least – but there's always something to see in Scotland: rowing under the colonies of silent puffins and the more vocal razorbills, shags and raucous guillemots; sailing in tandem with shearwaters and gannets; teased by passing minke whales; and air-punching the arrival of bow-riding dolphins. My guests know not to approach too close – however much they wish to abscond with a baby seal!

Already I can feel they, too, are making their own connections with this wild landscape and its wildlife.

EPILOGUE

I t's May 2022 and *Wilder Journeys* is beginning to take shape. I'm having a week's break from the computer, living in a tent in the Scottish Highlands and, unsurprisingly, sheltering from the rain. Correction: I'm now sharing my friend's tent since mine blew away on the first day when we tried pitching it next to a loch without any wind shelter. I watched it get dragged under by the combination of wind and water, the ominous mountains looking down, laughing at me.

Outside the tent, a mountain rescue team is looking for a missing person. They were not one of our group but someone who dared to brave the perilous bog alone, perhaps setting off in a moment of madness. The rescuers tell us they have been poking about in the loch and scouring the mountainside for days.

It's cold, it's wet. It's difficult to find dry wood for a fire. I wonder what we would do if we ran out of food here and couldn't get back? The valley is vast and dramatic, windswept and barren.

The other campers, sheltering in their own tents, are, like me, probably feeling that this is not quite how they'd pictured a week advertised as "an exploration of belonging and discovering the inner child". I had imagined frolicking in the hills with butterflies landing on us and rainbows in the skies.

During that week in Scotland, I gained an even deeper appreciation of, and respect for, those authors of *Wilder Journeys* who had really pushed themselves beyond their comfort zone. Clearly, pushing ourselves to our limits can remind us of who and what we really are. Everyone has a different comfort zone, and it's possible to challenge yours without having to cross an ocean or walk a continent. I managed to challenge mine through spending a week camping in gale-force winds and driving rain.

Sitting in base camp under a tarp, huddled by the fire, I reflected that reconnecting with our animal self is not all forest bathing and wild swimming in pleasant weather. A sobering thought: being alive and being an animal is about survival. Being interconnected is knowing your place and knowing that you are just part of a huge, complex ecosystem. There are many things out there that might kill us, and just by existing we are killing other beings unintentionally. Of course, those people who are growing food, who rely on subsistence, or who live in precarious situations at the mercy of the elements know this already, as do those with traditional wisdom cultures. However, many of us have become quite removed from our existential reality and from the hardships of survivalism, sometimes from a place of privilege and comfort, and sometimes from urbanization, colonialism or cultural loss.

Yet even those who don't have to face their existential reality on a daily basis are feeling a deep-rooted sense that something isn't quite right about the way we are living. Eco-anxiety is on the rise. People are angry about racism, colonialism, sexism and war.

For me, a young person living in these times, my eco-anxiety is very present and alive. I am questioning whether I want to have children and make choices about what I do based on fear of causing further harm to the biosphere. I also feel a call to the wild – the call that many of these authors felt – a call to reconnect with my instincts and to be able to follow them. I'd like us to rewild our culture, to transform our society to make it more nurturing and loving. Is there a reset button? I often wonder.

It was these feelings that urged me to collect these amazing stories – to inspire myself and, I hope, to inspire others. Feeling disconnected from the land and water is a difficult conundrum. There is so much healing and wisdom that we are missing out on.

I'm sure I'm not the only one who feels somewhat domesticated, wondering how long I would fare if I decided to live in the wild – to really embody my animal self.

To me, at least, it seems obvious that many of us need to move toward reconnection and change our worldviews to recognize our dependence on non-human beings and forces for survival. This is important for our own mental health – it's been proven time and time again that being outdoors, away from the city smog, be it in the ocean or with feet on the soil, can help people to feel better. It's also important for the health of the biosphere we rely on; we need to simplify our lives, to adapt our ways of being to bring certain humans off a pedestal and back down to earth. We also need to build resilience through challenging ourselves, so that we can adapt to changes in the environment and to our resources more easily. Hopefully, we as a species can all pull together collectively – we all need each other in this effort.

Where to begin? Well, this volume has given me a few ideas. I'm inspired to go on a long walking journey, to upskill myself with bushcraft, grow food, learn foraging and to help regenerate biodiversity – learning how humans can live within nature rather than seeing the two realms as somewhat separate. I also want to support organizations such as David Malana's Color the Water, among others (see Resources, opposite), that help encourage people who lack confidence or the means to go on their own journeys of connection, for those who feel that "nature" is not for them. We are all nature, both human and animal.

So my question for you is … where will your life take you next?

Tell us @wilder.journeys

Laurie King

RESOURCES

Wilder Journeys
www.wilderjourneys.com; @wilder.journeys

Contributors

Angela Maxwell: www.shewalkstheearth.com; @angelamariemaxwell
Bill Plotkin, Animas: www.animas.org
Camille Dungy: https://camilledungy.com; @camilledungy
Celia Bull, Selkie Explorers: www.selkie-explorers.com
David Malana, Color the Water: www.colorthewater.org
David Whyte: https://davidwhyte.com; @davidjwhyte
Denise Rowe, Earth Dances: www.earthdances.co.uk
Fatimah Asghar: www.fatimahasghar.com; @asgharthegrouch
Hamza Yassin: @hamzayassin90
Jennifer Joosten-Brisk: www.jenniferbrisk.com
Karen Darke: @handbikedarke
Laurie King: www.calloftheforest.co.uk
Lemn Sissay: www.lemnsissay.com; @sissaylemn
Lynx Vilden: www.lynxvilden.com
Miriam Lancewood: https://miriamlancewood.com
Roz Savage: www.rozsavage.com; @rozsavage
Rupert Marques: www.handontheearth.org
Selina Tusitala Marsh: @selinatusitalamarsh
Sophie Sung-Bin Hilaire: @sophiehilaire

Endorsers

Sir Chris Bonnington: www.bonington.com/

Ben Fogle: www.benfogle.com/

Oli Broadhead: www.olibroadhead.com/

Steve, The Happy Pear: https://thehappypear.ie/

Max Girardeau, The Visionaries: https://thevisionaries.org.uk/

Other organizations

UK

Backbone: www.backbone.uk.net

Explorers Connect: www.explorersconnect.com

Pendragon Project: www.pendragonproject.org

Alliance for Wild Ethics: https://wildethics.org/.

Verse in Dialog : https://verseindialog.com/

Stop Ecocide: www.stopecocide.earth

USA

Black People Who Hike: https://blackpeoplewhohike.com

Native Women's Wilderness: www.nativewomenswilderness.org

Mission Blue: https://mission-blue.org

Australia

Nature's Apprentice: www.naturesapprentice.com.au

Books by contributors

Adventure Revolution: The Life-changing Power of Choosing Challenge by Belinda Kirk

Woman in the Wilderness by Miriam Lancewood

Wild at Heart by Miriam Lancewood

Stop Drifting, Start Rowing: One Woman's Search for Happiness and Meaning Alone on the Pacific by Roz Savage

Rowing the Atlantic: Lessons Learned on the Open Ocean by Roz Savage

The Ocean in a Drop: Navigating from Crisis to Consciousness by Roz Savage

Out of the Forest by Gregory P Smith

The Walkabout Chronicles: Epic Journeys by Foot by Tor and Siffy Torkildson (chapter by Angela Maxwell)

Giant Steps by Karl Bushby

Boundless: An Adventure Beyond Limits by Karen Darke

If You Fall: It's a Beginning by Karen Darke

Soulcraft by Bill Plotkin

Becoming Animal by David Abram

The Hunter-Gatherer Way by Ffyona Campbell

Return: A Journey Back to Living Wild by Lynx Vilden

Other books

The Salt Path by Raynor Winn

Wild: An Elemental Journey by Jay Griffiths

Mississippi Solo by Eddy L Harris

Waymaking: An Anthology of Women's Adventure Writing, Poetry and Art edited by Helen Mort, Claire Carter, Heather Dawe, Camilla Barnard and Melissa Harrison

Over the Lip of the World: Among the Storytellers of Madagascar by Colleen J McElroy

Seaside Donkey by Hannah Engelkamp

Places by Robert Macfarlane

The Living Mountain by Nan Shepherd

Into the Wild by Jon Krakauer

Wild by Cheryl Strayed

My Year Without Matches: Escaping the City in Search of the Wild by Claire Dunn

Braiding Sweetgrass by Robin Wall Kimmerer

If Women Rose Rooted by Sharon Blackie

Journeys in the Wild: A Secret Life of a Cameraman by Gavin Thurston

ACKNOWLEDGEMENTS

To all the beings who have ventured with us on the wild journey of this creation – Thank You.

To all the contributors to this book, for being generous with time and wisdom, and for helping us make a dream a reality:

Angela Maxwell, Roz Savage, Rupert Marques, Jennifer Brisk, Celia Bull, Hamza Yassin, David Malana, Karl Bushby, Karen Darke, Gregory Smith, Denise Rowe, Sophie Hilaire, Belinda Kirk, Zena Edwards, Selina Tusitala Marsh, Lemn Sissay, Chloé Dyson, Lynx Vilden, Ffyona Cambell, Gabriella Garcia, Bill Plotkin, David Whyte, Fatimah Asghar and David Abram.

To all our endorsers and supporters.

To Lucy Carroll at Watkins Media UK, and to all the team behind the scenes, for believing in our idea and producing it.

Another shout out – Sarah King for her dedication to punctuation and spelling, and also to Oliver Gadsby for helping to make this happen.

Lastly, we must not forget all the trees, plants and animals that have contributed to the creation of this book.

Many thanks!